Alfonso Gálvez

THE MYSTERY
OF PRAYER

Translated from the Spanish by

Father Lope Pascual and Marcia K. Maranski

New Jersey

U.S.A. - 2025

CATALOGING DATA

Author: Gálvez, Alfonso, 1932–2022
Title: The Mystery of Prayer

First Printing   New Jersey, 2015
Second Printing   New Jersey, 2025

Library of Congress Control Number: 2025904257

ISBN: 978-1-953170-49-1
978-1-953170-50-7 (e-book)

**Published by
Shoreless Lake Press
P.O. Box 157
Stewartsville, New Jersey 08886**

This book is dedicated to the few still extant faithful who integrate the Catholic Church living in catacombs. Not the Church that is to come in the future, but the one which is already a reality among us.

PRELIMINARY NOTE OF THE AUTHOR

I was born to supernatural life within the Catholic, Apostolic, Roman Church, which I consider to be the one true Church founded by Jesus Christ; and I hope that God, in His goodness and mercy, will grant me the grace of dying in her bosom as her humble son.

Often one has to express or write things that need be repeated even if it is superfluous to say them. It would be unnecessary to insist on the following point as it becomes clear after reading the content of this book: I have tried at all times to be faithful to the centuries–old Doctrine of the Catholic Church contained in Sacred Scripture and Tradition and as it has always been interpreted by the Fathers and the Magisterium of the Church. If, notwithstanding this profession of faith, anything in this book is found to be contrary to this Doctrine, let it be considered as false and unsaid, as well as entirely alien to my intention and a mere product of my ignorance. Nevertheless, I consider it necessary to include this Preliminary Note in the English edition, for I neglected by accident to put it into the Spanish original.

As any fairly knowledgeable reader can notice, the content of this book is difficult, original in some aspects vis–à–vis what classical manuals have always stated and, consequently, open to discussion at least on some points. It must be added to this, as I admit in the book, that I lack the personal experience in regard to mystical prayer, which is another vulnerable element of this essay.

Nevertheless, I have a special interest in emphasizing some topics contained in this book.

First, it is not my intention to criticize or alter any doctrine of such outstanding mystics as Saint John of the Cross and Saint Teresa of Jesus, whom I admire and for whom I have always had a special fondness. I have only tried to present in a way more *accessible* and intelligible to modern man their doctrines as they have always been understood. It goes without saying that *accessible* does not mean adapted to modern trendy philosophies. I have merely attempted, in a more down–to–earth language generally used by modern man, to *present* doctrinal issues, without in the least bit changing their content, which were written more in accord with the language and the spirit of a particular age and which today may seem particularly difficult to understand and accept.

I have put special effort in trying to clarify some points of the doctrine of Saint John of the Cross with regard to the *Nights* of the senses and of the spirit whose unusual harshness may scare modern fainthearted souls. These souls, after all, belong to a world which long ago stopped believing in the advantage of practicing ascetic virtue, in the need for purification, for penance, for embracing the *narrow path* as the only roads leading to the Cross, veritable instruments of progress in prayer, of salvation, and of getting near to Jesus Christ.

Only in one matter do I express my manifest discrepancy with the doctrine of Saint John of the Cross. I am referring to his doctrine that it is absolutely necessary to abandon even the *notion* of the Humanity of Jesus Christ as an indispensable means to attaining a total identification with divine life in the highest degrees of prayer. But this issue is left open to the investigation of theologians and intellectuals; nevertheless, I clearly affirm that Saint John of the Cross is a Saint and a Doctor of the Church whereas I am merely an apprentice and an aficionado. That is why I take special care in admitting that there is a probable possibility that I either misunderstood the Saint or am totally wrong.

I want to emphasize even more that I and the doctrines of Illuminist, Pentecostal, Charismatic, and similar

Movements are poles apart. I think that their tenets have nothing to do with the Catholic Church for they are totally alien to the Truth. Personally, I have always felt a particular repugnance toward Illuminism and Charismatic Movements whose Gnostic and Protestant origins and procedures make them utterly repulsive. Every inspiration from the Spirit, or grace from On High, always transcends mere individual subjectivism and follows the paths of true Catholic Doctrine.

I think that I have stated very clearly in this book that nobody should dare to tread the difficult paths of mystical prayer who does not previously submit himself to a serious and sound spiritual director; that nobody should follow only his own personal criteria when it comes to *inspirations* which, after all, could very well be merely a product of one's imagination.

Finally, I do not try to impose my doctrine on anybody. The ideas expounded in this book are but my own *suggestions* offered to the criterion and personal reflection of good–willed individuals who think that they may deserve some consideration.

First Part

About Prayer

1. Introduction

First, I must caution the reader that everything I will say here will be solely concerned with mental prayer, except when occasionally I may expressly allude to vocal prayer.

I have intentionally begun the title of this chapter with the preposition *about*, for the sake of honesty and love of truth, and for no other reason. Talking about *prayer*, strictly prayer, is a practically impossible task. Any author who, even with the best of intentions, has undertaken the preparation of a treatise on prayer —and I am one of them— is far from suspecting that he will not go beyond a superficial level.

Regarding this task, the only expected probable outcome will be nothing short of roundabouts, circumlocutions, speculations, and technicalities that will attempt to say something but which will never be more than an approach to reality. Kind readers will believe that they have learned something; it is even possible that the book be a success with a vast audience willing to read it. The truth, however, is that explaining what the *essence* of prayer is and what goes on *in it* —or *within it*— is forbidden ground for average people, known only to those who, by the grace of God, tread on it.

It does not matter whether the author is convinced that he is talking about the essence of prayer or if naive readers think that they have acquired a bit of knowledge of something essential; in reality, both are merely circling the periphery of the subject.[1]

I have always been a great admirer and an ardent devotee of Saint Teresa of Avila —a true *fan*, in modern parlance. I have avidly read all her books, even as a teenager. Although I must confess that both *The Interior Castle* or *The Mansions* —which has always seemed to me the best book on prayer ever written (despite its depth, which made it very difficult for me to read)— and her *Autobiography* aroused my greatest enthusiasm.

Actually it was she who made me discover the fantastic and wonderful world —unknown to me until then— of what could be a loving relationship with God and the inexpressible dialogue of love between two lovers: God and man in this case. If dialogue between two human lovers

---

[1] Except if one of them receives the extraordinary graces of contemplative prayer from God; only he who practices and experiences true prayer can know it.

(within the scope of what is true love) is in itself ineffable and unintelligible to any outsider, then one could logically say that the dialogue between God and His creature would seem inaccessible and unimaginable to any human being. After many a year, I realized that this youthful intuition had landed squarely on the truth. Yet there was still too much progress for me to make to approach a light, which even now I can barely see in the distance, to finally come to the realization that I understood nothing yet...!

But this discovery was for me as if I had landed on another planet; so much so that life and the prospects of my existence took on an entirely new meaning from then on. For the youngster that I was, God had never been anything more than an Infinite and Good Being to Whom I could turn in any need; I found no difficulty in loving Him (in my own way), quite apart from the requirements of the First Commandment and caring about further demands that could complicate my life.

It was then that I suddenly discovered that God wanted to be my friend; that I could fall madly in love with Him, and that I could ravish His heart. This opened the doors of a world where I could enter and walk upon secluded paths trodden by lovers, undoubtedly murmuring to each other in whispers that which would be ineffable in itself to anyone else. Although all this was too intense for my mind and my heart, I found there the answer to the question I had often asked myself: *Does life have any meaning?* a question for which I had never found an answer.

Then I began to suspect that perhaps prayer could be the conduit to the wonderful and inexpressible madness of the *one-to-one* intimacy between God and His creature; nothing short of the splendid adventure of two ardent lovers whose love relationship and its inextricable secrets between them would be *impossible for them to transcribe.*

In effect, much later I realized that the intuitions of my youth were well founded, for it was really impossible to explain, in any way, how all this could be accomplished. *This is why I said earlier that it is impossible to speak of the essence of contemplative prayer or of what contemplative prayer consists.* I am convinced that spiritual writers have often *conned* their readers: explaining the various methods and procedures of prayer, its different kinds and elements, its corresponding place within the successive stages of the spiritual life, the difficulties that may arise and how to overcome them, etc., etc.; all of which, however, leaves us without knowing the true heart and the true secret of prayer. Indeed, not many people are willing to acknowledge that they are unable to unravel the contents of something whose true nature they either ignore or finally recognize as a mystery that is completely inaccessible to human understanding unless God provides it with special graces.

Now one can understand the amusing incident that happened to me in my youth with Saint Teresa of Jesus, my favorite saint for whom I feel so much affection. I had barely come of age when I first read *The Way of Perfection*. The book for me was a pleasant surprise that only increased as I started reading it and found that the Saint intended to explain what contemplative life was: Nothing less than *Contemplative Life*...! And with such a Teacher...! It seemed so wonderful; an incredible and unexpected gift! So right away I started to learn about and enjoy one of the mysteries that most intrigued and thrilled my heart. At last...!

The truth is that when a person is young he is willing to *believe anything*. The world looks wonderful and indicates that there is an abundance of goodness, beauty, and truth within it. Of course, when one grows older, he adopts a guarded approach, sometimes unconsciously, of believing nothing, or almost nothing, of what the world offers. Both attitudes are wrong, of course. Not everything is true and not everything is a lie; therefore, it is better to adopt an attitude of prudent caution that would allow the ability to exercise objective and sound judgment. And everything leads to the belief that we are better equipped to use this judgment when, through accumulated years, we have acquired a greater supply of wisdom and are more at ease to judge with confidence.

When the occurrence to which I am referring took place, I was rather young, as I said. So I did not hesitate for a moment to believe that I was finally to have access to the great secret that I had for so long wanted to know; I soon discovered that I was wrong. This is what happened.

As I went through the book, I grew increasingly impatient to learn about what mattered most to me, as the Saint had promised. But, to my disappointment, she became gradually more prolix in her explanations of the various petitions of the *Lord's Prayer*. Finally, I reached the end of the book, but contemplative prayer had never appeared anywhere! It was one of the many occasions on which the Saint of Ávila, my favorite saint, made me smile through her writings. That is why I am convinced that someday, trusting in the goodness of God, I will meet her in Heaven, and we will laugh together and discuss many of the things she has written about.[2] I admit that my innate

---

[2]In Heaven, according to Saint Thomas, the vision of the Satiating Truth will not leave much room for any clarification. But I think that, perhaps, at the heart of the Eternal Beatitude we will experience something similar to the feelings of the *hobbits*, as told in the saga of the immortal Tolkien: the pleasure of retelling and enjoying familiar stories, not to mention the reward and pleasure with which the fantasy of those interesting stories enrich our imagination.

suspiciousness and the natural inclinations of my personality have made me often doubt (of course affectionately) some of her sayings. Personally, I have many times enjoyed the suspicions contrived by my mischievous mind: Did the Saint really write the facts of her life only because her confessors *compelled* her, without exerting her influence —unconsciously, to be sure— on him to do so? Were her numerous *relapses* into her faults, forcing her to start over again, as severe and as frequent as she tells...? And so on. These wonderings, strangely enough, only increased my admiration and affection for this more than remarkable woman. Honesty, however, compels me to close this parenthesis by making a confession: of course it is true that I was never right regarding my foolish and loving suspicions. But what does the reader think? Was there some beneficial influence on her confessors, perhaps on occasion and without intending it, or some slight exaggeration in her insistence on her faults?

Anyway, I could not stop smiling when for the last time I closed *The Way of Perfection*. I could not help but establish an odd parallel between it and the famous poem *Jovial Supper* by Baltasar del Alcázar.[3]

---

[3]Baltasar del Alcázar (1530–1606) was a poet of the Spanish Golden Age. He served the Marquis of Santa Cruz and never had any intention of publishing his works. The Painter Francisco Pacheco copied the only extant manuscript and painted his portrait.

I would not want some ill–intentioned person to suspect any irreverence on my part toward Saint Teresa. It is just that there is a similarity of situations between the end of the book and the end of the poem, despite both works being so different in nature; which leads me to make a brief reference to the meal that Baltasar del Alcázar describes so jovially.

The poet begins by informing us that he resides in Jaén, a city where the gentleman Don Lope de Sosa, who has a Portuguese servant, has also set up camp. It turns out that this gentleman had undergone an interesting adventure that the poet was about to relate to his sister Inés, as he states in his famous lines:

> *And I'll tell you, Inés, about him,*
> *The most daring thing you have ever heard.*

Given the time of the day, however, the poet fancied first to start the meal that his sister had already prepared. This offered him the opportunity to describe, in a thorough and detailed manner, the most bountiful, plentiful, tantalizing, delightful, and exhilarating supper imaginable. Unfortunately, when it was over, time had passed and the clock chimed eleven at night, as is told:

> *Know, Inés, my sister*
> *That the Portuguese fell ill...*
> *The clock just struck eleven, I fall asleep,*
> *Let us postpone the story for tomorrow.*

And this was how both stories ended.

On the other hand, what could Saint Teresa explain? She had already said everything, exhausting all the potentialities of human language, in both *The Book of My Life* and *The Interior Castle*; in the latter, she makes a tedious description —difficult to grasp for those not long initiated into the mystery of prayer— of the intricate and tortuous paths that lead to the innermost dwellings of that fortress.

2. Contemplative Prayer

The few phrases of her conversations with God which Saint Teresa mentions in her works, especially the words addressed by God to her, could be termed, so to speak, as *occasional language*; a language generally destined to dispel the Saint's fears or to take care of some business rather than to describe the intimate conversation between the two of them.

The fact is that the dialogue of love —most particularly and above all divine–human dialogue— is *completed* and *ends* once it has been listened to by each of the two lovers: in our case, God and His creature.[4] What each lover says to the other would be unintelligible to anyone outside their relationship. Love is inaccessible to *third parties* because love is the most intimate and essentially *personal* reality there is, carried out between an *I* and a *thou* and embracing the love which unites them.[5]

This Dialogue thus becomes the paradigm of any communication among men, but only if it turns out to be a *second analogate* or a second or third degree analogate. And collective Dialogue, in turn, only makes sense and is effective when it is based on the previous ones. This is the reason for the failure of the *dialogue* so insistently

---

[4]Any human loving dialogue, even when it is animated by the best and truest love, has divine–human dialogue as its first analogate and, therefore, as its reference point. Thus, divine–human dialogue becomes the only arena where man is allowed to participate, in some way, in the mysterious and eternal Dialogue of Love taking place in the Bosom of the Trinity. As one can easily understand, we are referring exclusively to divine–human dialogue; or, simply, to what we have agreed to call contemplative prayer.

[5]In this sense, love should always be between two persons, reciprocal and bilateral. Essential Love, however, is Tri–Personal because the bond uniting Father and Son is also a Person. A creature can only have a relationship with the Father through his intimate and direct relationship of friendship with the Son, brought about, in turn, by the guidance of the inductor–conductor Wire, the Holy Spirit.

belabored in the world and in the church, and so often regarded as the magical instrument for solving all possible human divergences.

Some attributes of true dialogue are beautifully expressed in this verse uttered by the bride:

> *My Love, Stars in the Heavens,*
> *Seas kissed by bows of a thousand ships below,*
> *Eyes of sweet youthful maidens,*
> *Songs of wood thrush and sparrow,*
> *Everything I told you and which you now know.*[6]

Everything I told you and which you now know. Indeed, because only the beloved person, to whom this compliment is addressed, can hear it and understand it. Otherwise this expression of love would lose its intimacy, its secrecy,

---

[6]In this edition, the poems of the text have been cited according to the updated version of them in Alfonso Gálvez, *Cantos del Final del Camino*, Shoreless lake Press, 2020, (from now on *CFC*). For this stanza, *CFC* 67. In the Spanish original:

> *Mi Amado, las estrellas,*
> *el mar que besan proas de mil naves,*
> *los ojos de doncellas,*
> *el canto de las aves,*
> *aquello que te dije y que tú sabes.*

as well as the mystery of its essence: even the content itself. The dialogue of love, always and in every instance, is addressed by an *I* to a *thou* and reciprocally answered. It cannot be otherwise.

Indeed, as happens in any relationship of love, the lover surrenders himself *totally and integrally* to the beloved, and vice–versa.[7] Besides, any other relationship of love (alien to the divine–human relationship of love) would be essentially impossible, at least as far as its total perfection is concerned —legitimate loving relationships: conjugal, father–son, fraternal, between friends... Contrarily, intrinsically perverse interactions in general (sprung from false love) and those referred to as *disordered affections* — or similar ones— by spiritual and ascetical writers cannot be considered as loving relationships.

Hence the fact, so often analyzed, that in the divine-human relationship of love the creature ardently seeks silence and solitude, once he has been given the grace of contemplative prayer; for it is absolutely true that *both*

---

[7]God, Infinite and Perfect Being, can give Himself totally to every individual human being, but man cannot do the same in any relationship that he may maintain; hence, the command is needed: *Thou shalt love the Lord thy God with thy whole heart and with thy whole strength.*

are necessary[8] in order for this prayer to occur, as the following verse suggests:

> *Following shepherds and sheep,*
> *I wandered to where I knew my Love would be*
> *Hidden in hillsides so deep;*
> *And he spoke to me softly*
> *But the breezes stole his whispered words from me.*[9]

Notice that both lovers, despite their solitude, speak in *whispers*. This detail is far from being insignificant or merely poetic. In effect, the conversation of love — as usual, we refer to divine–human love— deplores voices

---

[8] The instances of *rapture* —as she generally names it— that Saint Teresa recounts and which, despite herself, occurred in public, are extraordinary exceptions that God, in His mysterious plans, rarely allows. Apropos of which it should be noted that it is necessary to monitor the possibility of false mystical phenomena, as may occur with *levitation* for example. The devil sometimes uses them to deceive gullible souls who, precisely because they lack humility, are not likely to subject themselves to the strict control of a good spiritual director.

[9] *CFC*, 6. In the Spanish original:

> *Siguiendo a los pastores,*
> *llegué adonde el Amado me esperaba*
> *oculto en los alcores;*
> *y, mientras que me hablaba,*
> *el aire sus susurros aventaba.*

that can be heard, noises or drum rolls constantly swarming around. Compliments of love need be *insinuated* rather than heard; with two provisos:

First, *insinuation* does not mean in the least a lack of clear communication, rather just the opposite. Let us remember that poetry, for example, is able to *say*, express, and touch heights that human language and mere prose cannot begin to *reach*.

Second, the compliments of love have *need of silence* to be pronounced. Let us not forget that communication is more perfect through silence than through words. Words is the usual means of communication proper to human nature, perfectly adapted to its essence but not the most perfect (angels, for example, need no words to communicate with one another). In the Bosom of the Trinity, the Father *tells* Himself what He is with only one Word; and in that Word He says *all*; and, according to Saint John of the Cross, He has also told us *everything* we need to know through His Word.

Saint Teresa speaks often of raptures and ecstasies in which God communicated to her what is ineffable *with a total absence of words* as human language understands them. Saint Paul writes that he was caught up into the third heaven, where he heard unspeakable words (*arcana*

verba) which it is not lawful for man to utter.[10] It seems
logical to suppose that the Apostle referred to words that
cannot be expressed by means of human language, since
entirely heavenly things do not fit within the limits of
human expression and communication. No doubt God
uses extraordinary means, totally unknown to us, when
He wants to dialogue and communicate intimate secrets
of His Heart to chosen souls. On the other hand, what
Saint Teresa is referring to has been well confirmed by the
witness of other mystics, such as Saint John of the Cross.

Do not think that I have inadvertently neglected to mention the
testimony of other mystics, Saint John of the Cross for example. Actually I have done so deliberately, since this essay about mystical prayer
has no other purpose than to express my admiration for those chosen
souls to whom the grace of knowing and practicing it has been granted.
Therefore, I have tried to make its reading uncomplicated, even sim-
plified whenever possible, more accessible to the preferences and the
mentality of modern man.

Nevertheless, it is worth noting —for those who are fond of historical curiosities— that the renowned Hans Urs von Balthasar has
heretofore mentioned important differences between the spirituality of
Saint John of the Cross and that of Saint Teresa. Moved by curiosity
and by a sincere devotion to both saints, I endeavored to study the
distinctions directly from this author (although I do not hold him in
any great esteem), both in his work *The Glory of the Lord: A Theological Aesthetics* and less so in his *The Contemplative Prayer*; my

---

[10]2 Cor 12: 2–4.

memory does not serve me well, given the many intervening years. I had the opportunity of reading the former in French when the Spanish translation was not yet available (*La Gloire et la Croix. Les Aspects Esthétiques de la Révélation*, Les Éditions du Cerf, Paris, 1993, 8 volumes). When I finally read the Spanish version, the book seemed to me to be completely objectionable, a veritable web of deceit to the reader.

Truth be told, I had also previously noted an apparent contradiction between certain points of both mystical spiritualities, which impressed me indeed; hence my concern over this issue.

Ultimately, however, I realized that the differences are circumstantial and, above all, methodological. Despite the fact that some of them are certainly important, those differences in no way affect the essential and fundamental doctrine. It could not be otherwise, since both are Doctors of the Church: two Spanish glories and pinnacles of mysticism for the good of the Universal Church.

The verse we are analyzing also explains that, as the Beloved speaks to the bride, *the breezes stole his whispered words from me.* This detail cannot be attributed to chance. As the Bridegroom addresses His declarations of love to the bride, and taking into account that she was their only recipient and that *only she could hear and understand them*, once uttered, the wind took them, for it did not make any sense for those proclamations of love to be in any place other than the heart and memory of the beloved.

Another feature of the mystical life, quite often present in contemplative prayer, has to do with stops and even set-backs along the road[11] —in addition to which the absence of the Bridegroom that the soul in love, to her own torment, is forced to suffer. It is of very little importance for the soul whether the setbacks and *absences of the Beloved* so often mentioned by Saint Teresa are real or perceived; she always feels them as absolutely authentic. No doubt they are phases of the educational process used by God to purify and ease the road of those souls whom He loves. Nevertheless, these phases cannot but bring about in those souls a deep torment, which, by paradox and according to testimony of the mystics themselves, is frequently extremely joyful. One must admit that God's ways are incomprehensible, even though we know that they always lead to the good of His chosen ones.

As we have repeatedly said, given the loftiness of this topic, poetry is more capable than prose to *explain* it, for poetry can instill in the human heart feelings and intuitions that merely everyday human language cannot. That is why I have chosen another verse in trying to say some-

---

[11]Particularly in order to avoid discouragement in beginners, Saint Teresa insists on the numerous and alternating progressions and set-backs found along the difficult road leading to the highest point of intimacy with God.

thing about the absences of the Bridegroom; undoubtedly
a recurrent theme in mystical life that ultimately results
in phenomena and situations too mysterious for beginners;
merely undertaking this effort may lead one to think that
I am being daring and presumptuous:

> *In your orchard a small bird,*
> *In grief at your absence, sang with a sad sound;*
> *And, when your soft voice she heard,*
> *Quickly rose up from the ground,*
> *To search in her swift flight where you would be found.*[12]

The bride is undergoing total solitude in the grip of
deep sorrow because of the absence of the Beloved; suddenly, she is joyfully surprised at hearing the unmistakable
voice of the Bridegroom Who is calling her and seemingly
approaching her:

---

[12] *CFC*, 9. In the Spanish original:

> *De tu vergel un ave*
> *por tu ausencia cantaba en desconsuelo;*
> *y oyó tu voz suave*
> *y, alzándose del suelo,*
> *a buscarte emprendió veloz su vuelo.*

> *The voice of my beloved! Behold, he cometh*
> *Leaping upon the mountains,*
> *Skipping upon the hills.*
> *My beloved is like a roe or a young hart.*
> *Behold, he standeth behind our wall,*
> *He looketh forth at the windows,*
> *Shewing himself through the lattice.*
> *Behold, my beloved speaketh to me:*[13]

Surprise and joy in the small bird are followed by her sudden decision of going out to meet Him as quickly as possible, for she is urged by longing and hope of seeing her desire at long last fulfilled, as the verse says: *To search in her swift flight where you would be found.*

In a similar context, in chapter twenty of her *Life* Saint Teresa refers to Psalm 55, which goes like this:

> *And I said: Who will give me wings like a dove*
> *And I will fly and be at rest?*[14]

Rest for her can be provided only by intimacy with God: the only place of joyful repose there can be.

---

[13]Sg 2: 8–10.
[14]Ps 55:7.

And *swift flight* is always involved, for love is by nature impatient and hasty; more impatient and hasty than anything else in the entire world if we are referring to divine–human love. And because it is extremely difficult for the soul to endure a waiting that prolongs the absence of the Beloved, she goes out in haste, searching for Him —with the greatest haste— when she perceives, at last, that He is getting closer.

Hence, the desire to experience death together with Christ is essential to Christian existence and not merely to mystic life. Thus, Saint Paul says: *But I am strained between the two, having a desire to be dissolved and to be with Christ, a thing by far the better. But to abide still in the flesh is more needful for you.*[15] This waiting, as happens to anything that belongs to the supernatural realm and, much more so, to the mysterious and unknown paths leading to the most intimate and greatest depths of the Heart of God, has an ambivalent nature that, being ineffable, cannot be explained.

Indeed, this waiting involves, on the one hand, tormenting longings caused by the absence of the beloved person (God, in the case of the soul). On the other, because this waiting knows that it is destined to end, it feeds

---

[15]Phil 1: 23–24.

on the ardent desire to possess the beloved person, to anticipate more and more his presence. His momentary absence, as lovers are well aware, works as an incentive to increase love as the absence prolongs. Here is another strange and inexplicable paradox of love: the lovers want to be together at the earliest possible moment; at the same time, and if possible, they would wish that the cause that ignites ever stronger the flames of their love and feeds their expectation may last incessantly, regardless of time, until it becomes a devouring fire quite capable of reducing the lover to ashes, for he cannot understand love differently: *For our God is a consuming fire.*[16] Alluding to this reality, Saint Teresa said:

> *I die because I do not die.*

The voice of the Beloved —which is inaudible, unintelligible, and ineffable to all others— calls the soul and attracts her with unutterable impetus: *The Spirit himself maketh intercession for us with groaning which cannot be uttered.*[17] Here the very divine Word admits Itself unable to express all It wants to say. For love speaks through the

---

[16]Heb 12:29.
[17]Rom 8:26.

heart, but rarely finds ways to explain itself by means of the mouth. The bride, in the following stanza, expresses this same reality with an equivalent language which is, nevertheless, peculiar to poetry:

> *My Bridegroom's voice is for me,*
> *Like the wake of a ship deeply furrowing*
> *Like winds that stir so lightly*
> *Like a gentle whispering,*
> *Like the solemn moves of a night bird on wing.*[18]

The path leading to the meeting of the lovers is long and tiresome, filled with waiting moments and unexpected stops, longings, and absences, but is also animated by the anticipation of a joyful waiting that knows that, one day, it will find what it is looking for:

---

[18] *CFC*, 75. In the Spanish original:

> *Es la voz del Esposo*
> *como la huidiza estela de una nave,*
> *como aire rumoroso,*
> *como susurro suave,*
> *como el vuelo nocturno de algún ave.*

Bleak winter has finished its cycle and passed;
Spring flowers display true signs of life at last,
And now the woods are filled with sweet scents and trills
And the lark flies from deep valley to the hills.

In search of your footprints, I follow the trail
Which rises uphill from the long and deep vale
And in pain I suffer when yourself you hide
And to my sad complaints you have not replied.

And in the soft mellowing evenings of spring
As if once more by your side I were lying
In the warm shade of the forest of pine trees
I hear the sad lark in her sorrow she grieves.[19]

---

[19] *CFC*, 28. In the Spanish original:

> *Ya el gélido invierno su ciclo fenece,*
> *cuando en primavera sus flores ofrece*
> *y el bosque se llena de trinos y aromas*
> *al par que la alondra vuela hacia las lomas.*
>
> *Buscando tus huellas voy por el sendero*
> *que del hondo valle sube hasta el otero;*
> *y sufro de angustias al ver que te escondes*
> *y a mis tristes quejas Tú ya no respondes.*
>
> *Y en las suaves tardes de la primavera,*
> *como si a tu lado de nuevo estuviera,*
> *entre los pinares, a su tibia sombra,*
> *el lamento escucho de la triste alondra.*

But a moment arrives when the small bird can no longer wait and she makes a supreme effort to fly off and arrive as soon as possible to where her Beloved is waiting for her.

She will always come up against the difficult struggle to see whose impatience is stronger. The precise moment of the death of the saints, and why they died exactly then, will remain hidden for now in the heart of God. Why do some chosen and blessed souls die young, while others must walk the path of a long life? Only God knows, but one thing is certain: one and the other will fly to Heaven *when God's loving impatience can no longer wait.*

And thus:

...And waiting no longer the bird took to wing
In search of her Loved One, her Friend, her Dearest,
Leaving forever her comfort, her soft nest,
Without any grief, nor pain, nor sorrowing.[20]

But one soon realizes that, at the bottom of this issue, we are always circling around the same thing. Our long-

---

[20] *CFC*, 79. In the Spanish original:

...Y ya sin esperar alzó su vuelo
en busca del Amado tan querido,
dejando para siempre el viejo nido
sin pena, ni dolor, ni desconsuelo.

ing to know the mysterious essence of the world of love relationships with God makes us speak, again and again, of the conditions under which this divine–human relationship of love operates, exists, and develops: the search for solitude, for example, the fundamental role of silence, the detachment from created things... and all other circumstances that one may want to add, for this topic is vast in depth and breadth. And yet, we never reach the essential, what we are most interested in knowing: the unknown underlying principles, the mysterious *essence* of the divine–human relationship of love, as well as the real content of what both lovers *say* to each other. We know quite well that we are dealing with a theme off–limits, *a fountain sealed up*[21] to strangers; which cannot impede the innate desire that every man feels in his heart, whether he admits it or not, of finding God.

The divinely inspired book *Song of Songs* is the only work I know which contains a real conversation between lovers within the intimacy of a divine–human relationship of love.

This book is much more than a simple narration of a dialogue of love; it is the result of the mutual passion and total self–surrender that takes place in the divine–human

---

[21]Sg 4:12.

love relationship. This book reveals all the phases and moments of mystical life as we know it: absence of the Bridegroom and ensuing search of Him by the bride; advances and setbacks of the bride in her love relationship with her Bridegroom; their mutual longings for meeting and contemplating each other; both lovers *being on the same level*: a situation which is an essential element of love and which sometimes impels the Bridegroom to implore the bride to let Him enter her chambers and to be near her... Given a closer look, this book contains the entire foundation and essence of Christian mysticism, encompassing its different stages.

But this topic is more complicated than it seems. What we have said so far merely places us on the threshold of a deep mystery. In effect, the *Song of Songs*, given the subject it deals with and that it is an inspired book, raises a whole host of important issues rarely ever analyzed and worked out to the satisfaction of human understanding. We will try to list some of them here and advance various answers; we are well aware, however, that we can only speculate about mysteries that *are real* because they have been revealed, but which will always exceed our capabilities *until the day dawns and the morning star rises in your hearts,*[22] which is tantamount to saying until those mysteries can be contemplated under the light of God. Someone may question the reason behind their being revealed if their meaning will never be comprehended; let us remember that we are referring here to a merely relative intellection of those mysteries. At any rate, their content will always be somehow profitable for our souls, for that is why they have been revealed.

The first problem to be faced regarding the *Song of Songs* is the incontrovertible fact that God is restricted to the forms and modes of human language when He wants to communicate with man; which, at first sight, seems to simply agree with the limitations imposed by the nature of things. Should God want to be understood by man, He must comply with the natural human condition.

This brings to the forefront another issue, since we are talking about an inspired book: the various degrees of intellection that man can reach in the understanding of its mysteries.[23]

---

[22]2 Pet 1:19.

[23]God can reveal whatever He wants, even in an extraordinary way, as He indeed does to certain souls whom He chooses according to His designs; here we are talking in general, for no one will question that the *Song of Songs* has been inspired for the benefit of all men.

The limitations imposed by language is but one of many problems. We are facing the absorbing difficulty of the infinitely abysmal distance between God and man, now augmented and worsened because of sin and its consequences for a creature who had been destined in the beginning, by pure grace, to share the very nature of God.

It is true that God intervened in favor of man through the Incarnation and Redemption. But man's faculties remain weak, and he obstinately maintains this abyss of separation with his personal sins; consequently, despite grace and abundant divine help, man is forced to wage a constant battle between the spirit and the flesh which he must win in order to achieve his salvation.

The *Song of Songs*, as all inspired books, has to use human language, which is a *wall of contention*, a *barrier–filter*, placed between everything that God *says* there and what man can *understand*. The difference is enormously important, and it is more noticeable in this particular case because we are directly talking about divine–human love (despite its use of poetic and metaphoric ways, which are, after all, most adequate). Later we will deal with this topic at greater length. Now, it will suffice to say that this characteristic of the *Song of Songs* is what leads many *experts* and exegetes to interpret it as a mere collection of epithalamic songs.

Although we will not make any marginal comments on the trends of modern theology (fully imbued as it is with Modernism), which tends to explain everything pertaining to the supernatural order by natural means more acceptable to today's man, let us point out that these experts have forgotten what is most important and fundamental in this case without which the inspired *Song of Songs* would not make any sense and would be impossible to understand:

The theme of this book is love, specifically the Love of God freely offered to man. Its acceptance by the latter is what gives rise to the relations of divine–human love, which in the most outstanding cases go to levels of depth that reach the realm of mystical experience and contemplative prayer.

Given that love is the highest, most sublime, and most mysterious reality that exists in the visible and invisible universe, talking about it with even only a partial chance of success is undertaking a very risky endeavor.[24] And if we add the fact that Love is God (1 Jn 4:8), then we need Faith so as to approach Love in a way that excludes errors.

---

[24]One must admire the efforts of the Classics to explain love. Plato's *Dialogues*, which can justly be considered one of the paramount works written by man, achieves high levels of notable findings about love which, unfortunately, are mixed with reproachable and abysmal errors.

For only from love can one speak of love. And because true love is always a participation in divine love (otherwise it is not love), then only those who love can know God; which, in turn, is the only way to know something about love: *He who loveth not knoweth not God; for God is love.*[25] Consequently, approaching the *Song of Songs* without being animated by the love of God would be a more difficult undertaking than trying to read an old Chinese manuscript without having the slightest knowledge of this language.

Man's great tragedy is that he rebelled against God. This caused such monumental damage that the incredible price to be paid for its reparation could be provided only by God through His infinite Wisdom and Power. Thereupon, only two possibilities are left for man: freely and willingly to answer affirmatively to the Love offered to him by God or to reject it. Either option must be freely desired and accepted, as demanded by love's nature. These alternatives lead to either Eternal Joy or Eternal damnation.[26]

---

[25] 1 Jn 4:8.

[26] Given current events, everything seems to indicate that the majority of men are opting for the second possibility (Mt 7:14). The general apostasy that today's Church is suffering is surely providing Hell with a number of damned so great that the mercy of God hides it from us.

However it would be a grave mistake to assume that those who choose God's Love are driven by a particular consideration of what is most convenient. Such a thing would destroy the nature of true love: *true love is chosen only because of love.* A true lover —especially if we refer to divine–human love— does not choose the other party of the relationship for his own personal interest, about which he does not care at all; moreover, he would be willing to lose everything, including his own life and his own existence: *If any man come to me, and hate not his father and mother and wife and children and brethren and sisters, yea and his own life also, he cannot be my disciple.*[27]

This choice will turn into a long and difficult road for those who, enjoying special graces from God, reach the highest levels within the divine–human relationship of love; precisely there where the most inexplicable and extraordinary paradoxes occur.

On the one hand, the love of God, specified in a direct and intimate relationship with the Person of Jesus Christ,

---

[27]Lk 14:26; cf Mt 10:39; 16:25. According to Catholic Doctrine, a member of the faithful can also achieve salvation by recovering the lost grace through repentance caused by imperfect love (fear of hell, for example), which is called *attrition* to differentiate it from perfect contrition. Attrition also needs sacramental confession in order to be efficacious.

is made manifest along with the ineffable joy of the tender and personal friendship with God. On the other hand, this situation is accompanied by a number of trials and sufferings whose intensity would be difficult (not to say almost impossible) to describe here. Nevertheless, eliminating these sufferings is what the soul in love with God would least desire.

Thus, a Christian should never forget that when we are dealing with real lovers and people truly in love with God, any possible mention of *death out of love* has nothing to do with metaphor or mere literature.

But in both situations the *Song of Songs* expresses itself with its habitual depth and poetic beauty, as can be seen in those passages where the Bridegroom, filled with concern and love for His bride, tries to prevent anything from disturbing her:

> *I adjure you, O ye daughters of Jerusalem,*
> *By the roes, and the harts of the field,*
> *That you stir not up, nor make the beloved to awake,*
> *Till she pleases.*[28]

Saint John of the Cross glosses these verses with his own poetry which is also endowed with a delightful charm that flows from the unquenchable spring of beauty contained in the divine verses, as in those of the *Song of Songs*:

---

[28]Sg 2:7; 3:5.

> *You birds with airy wings,*
> *Lions, and stags, and roebucks leaping light,*
> *Hills, valleys, creeks, and springs,*
> *Waves, winds, and ardours bright,*
> *And things that rule the watches of the night:*
>
> *By the sweet lyre and call*
> *Of sirens, now I conjure you to cease*
> *Your tumults one and all,*
> *Nor echo on the wall*
> *That she may sleep securely and at peace.*[29]

The superhuman heights reached by the poetry of Saint John are a diamond extracted from the ore of precious stones that is as deep and abundant as unending divine Love.[30] Four centuries have passed and the poetry of this

---

[29]Saint John of the Cross, *Spiritual Canticle.*

[30]Scholars and experts in poetic art have been trying for centuries to explain the mystery of this poetry. Of course, always starting from merely natural and ordinary elements such as the genius of the poet from Fontiveros, the advantage provided by the historical moment in which he lived, and the like. These experts consider that Saint John's poetry has used as instruments nothing but procedures and techniques of the human arts; which in this case are nothing more than the poetic literature produced so far by man. As could not be otherwise, they have never achieved sufficient and satisfactory results.

holy Carmelite has not been bettered, nor even matched, by any other poetic composition in Castilian language. The reason being that although the diamond ore is still the same *there are no workers willing to descend the depths of the mine shafts to extract it.* And yet, the generosity of God is not diminished and He is always willing to bestow His gifts; as the prophet Isaiah says, *Ecce non est abbreviata manus Domini.*[31] The poetry of Saint John of the Cross is a reflection of the depth of beauty and love contained in the Heart of God; a glimpse of the infinite radiance that has been extracted in turn from the same work of the divine Poet as reflected in the *Song of Songs.* But this poetry is also a tangible demonstration of the reality of another mysterious challenge posed by the holy book, to which we have already alluded. For the hidden content of the verses of this Book can give rise to *fear and trembling* in him who is able to discover it; fear and trembling that are but the corollary of Perfect Joy as the human heart would be able to feel it: partially for now, but destined to become total in Eternal Life: *But when that which is perfect is come, that which is in part shall be done away with.*[32]

---

[31] Is 59:1.

[32] 1 Cor 13:10.

We have established, therefore, that the verses of the *Song of Songs*, while expressing in their beautiful poetic language what God wants to tell us about the mystery of the divine–human love relationship, they also *work as a veil that hides the total depth of the content of this relationship.* It could not be otherwise. First because, as we have said, this lofty reality is actually known (although partially) only by those privileged souls which have been chosen by God to experience the deep realities of mystical life and contemplative prayer. Second, because even God has to abide by the limitations of human language if He wants to be understood by man.

Nevertheless, it is astonishing to consider that these words of Jesus Christ, *I will not now call you servants; for the servant knoweth not what his lord doth. But I have called you friends, because all things, whatsoever I have heard of my Father, I have made known to you,*[33] have been understood by man as if referring to a merely fraternal affection. It seems that we never come to realize that when God says that He loves us as *friends* it is because He really considers us His *friends*; but in such a deep and intimate way as no human being has ever been able to find

---

[33] Jn 15:15.

in the true meaning of this beautiful word; even more so and especially when this word is pronounced by the mouth of God.

We have also said that the *Song of Songs* is a compendium of all the phases and contingencies that make up the fabric of mystic life, and more specifically of contemplative prayer. Let us remember but a few examples.

The longing and passionate search for the Bridegroom by the bride already appears at almost the very outset of the inspired Book:

> *Shew me, O thou whom my soul loveth,*
> *Where thou feedest, where thou liest in the midday,*
> *Lest I begin to wander*
> *After the flocks of thy companions.*[34]

This search, because it is not crowned with success, reaches moments of profound and sorrowful sentiments that become even bitter and extremely distressful. Actually everything is a reflection of what happens in a soul that sincerely seeks God but sees that her life is being

---

[34]Sg 1:7.

spent as if her fate were to seek but not find God; always invigorated by the hope that this not finding is *for the time being* destined to become *until now*. And so we have arrived in our analysis at one of the most *tragic* and inexplicable moments associated with the feelings that inundate the soul in love with God: she experiences the painful and unbearable absence of God, which compels her to the undertaking of eagerly trying to find Him as soon as possible:

> *I will rise, and will go about the city:*
> *In the streets and the broad ways*
> *I will seek him whom my soul loveth;*
> *I sought him, and I found him not.*
> *The watchmen who keep the city, found me:*
> *Have you seen him, whom my soul loveth?*[35]

Human poetry, in its own way and with all its limitations, tries to say the same thing:

---

[35]Sg 3: 2–3.

I looked but found you nowhere,
I called you with no reply;
When at last I saw you there,
I fainted with loving sigh.

I now live in darkness bleak
Nostalgia's pain holds me bound,
And from love so wounded weak
I die... you I have not found.

Have you heard my moans and tears...?
Has my sorrow, as I grieve,
Borne on wings of winds that breathe,
Come to you or reached your ears...?[36]

---

[36] *CFC*, 29. In the Spanish original:

Te busqué, mas no te hallé,
te llamé, mas no te oí,
y cuando al fin te encontré,
por tu amor desfallecí.

En la oscuridad he vivido
de nostalgia alimentado,
y tan de amores herido
que muero, pues no te he hallado.

¿Oíste al fin mis gemidos...?
¿Por fin mi triste lamento,
llevado en alas del viento,
ha llegado a tus oídos...?

One has to admire the struggle undergone by language —with an effort bordering on anguish— in its attempt to express what is impossible to say in any way whatsoever. Tremendous effort, to no avail, that involves both man and God Himself.

On the other hand, someone might be surprised, perhaps even shocked, by the *forceful* expressions used in the *Song of Songs*, and from the very beginning. For example, the desire expressed by the bride with respect to her Husband:

> *Let him kiss me with the kisses of his mouth:*
> *For thy love is better than wine.*[37]

This expression is so unrefined —*Let him kiss me with the kisses of his mouth*, or alternately, *Kiss me with the kisses of your mouth*— that it seems to not hesitate to use the most enticing expressions used by merely human lovers... But, truth be told, if one really wants to refer to the passionate love that the soul feels toward God, how better and clearer could it have been said so that man could understand?

---

[37]Sg 1:2.

True, this is not easy to comprehend by those who have never understood the love of God for man. They may think of God, but they imagine Him as an Infinite (also in distance, regarding us), Omnipotent, Supreme Judge... Nevertheless, they have never believed in Love without limits, Who, despite everything, wants man to share His intimate life and His own Love. He became one of us for that very purpose; hence all the consequences of the mystery of the Incarnation of the Word upon which only a few men have seriously reflected.

In the divine–human love relationship there are situations that are scarcely known —except possibly in their initial phase— by merely human love. But in mystical prayer, given the dignity of the divine Lover, these situations reach depths such as are impossible to explain with human language. One of the phenomena of contemplative prayer which, with the help of grace, has reached a high degree of perfection is the situation of *parity* or equality between God and the soul. Now, if the divine–human love relationship is the intimacy of the *face to face* between the two lovers...; if by mutual self–surrender each lover becomes the possession of the other in such a way that everything that belongs to the one belongs also to the other, which leads to an exchange and full communion of lives where either lover is no longer higher or lower;

> *My beloved is mine, and I am his*
> *He feedeth among the lilies.*

....

> *I am my beloved's,*
> And his desire is toward me.[38]

then there is no wonder that the divine Lover implores His bride to open the door and allow Him to approach her:

> *Open to me, my sister, my love,*
> *My dove, my undefiled;*
> *For my head is full of dew,*
> *And my locks of the drops of the night.*[39]

Here we are beginning to tread on the threshold of a universe that man could never have imagined. If a situation of loving intimacy between merely human lovers produces ardent feelings of excitement and happiness whose levels of intensity were so far unknown to them..., contemplative prayer becomes, more forcefully, a divine human relationship of love opened to a different world filled with

---

[38] Sg 2:16; 7:11.

[39] Sg 5:2.

mysteries on a level different from the merely human one, and where nothing at all can be explained. Within this new world, any reference to what is purely human, including relationships of love, becomes, in the mind and in the heart of the creature, only a remembrance whose entity does not go beyond being a simple *analogate*, so distant that it seems an insignificant thing vanishing in time and tending to nothingness.

It is thus essential to consider the way through which the creature establishes his relationship with God, Who is none other than *the Person of Jesus Christ Himself.*

This is a principle of transcendental importance for the whole of Humanity which has been mysteriously ignored by *all and sundry.* Jesus Christ said of Himself: *I am the way, and the Truth, and the Life; no one cometh to the Father, but by me.*[40] These are clear, firm, forceful words, absolutely incompatible with ambiguity and leaving no room for the slightest doubt. Countless efforts have been made —now more than ever— to hide, conceal, manipulate, and even kill them. Needless to say, those attempts have been a complete failure as the immutable promise of our Lord Himself assures us: *Heaven and earth shall pass away; but my words shall not pass away.*[41]

Saint John the Evangelist confirms and emphasizes his Master's words: *Who is a liar, but he who denieth that Jesus is the Christ? This is Antichrist, who denieth the Father and the Son. Whosoever denieth*

---

[40] Jn 14:6.

[41] Mk 13:31; Lk 21:33.

the Son, the same hath not the Father. He that confesseth the Son hath the Father also.[42]

But Judaism and Islam have not only rejected Jesus Christ, they have also *blocked* the road, preventing all access to Him. Thus these religions not only *do not have* Jesus Christ, but they have deliberately, with an iron will, filled all roads leading to Him with obstacles, making them *impassable.*

Therefore, according to a clear sentence from Revelation itself, *Judaism and Islam have not the Father,* which is tantamount to affirming that they *have not God either.* The Apostle Saint John goes even further and does not hesitate to call them *Antichrist.*

These are the plain, convincing, and clear facts as stated by the revealed Word of God. Unless one also wants, as a last and desperate resort, to deny the truth of the words contained in the Books of Revelation. In effect, the Modernist theology of the New Church has not hesitated to use this procedure, not realizing —intentionally not realizing— that once Revelation has been rejected, Faith has been deprived of any basis. Consequently, this Modernist theology has given rise to a purely natural religion without supernatural foundation, made by man, and resulting in a Humanity without God on the verge of its own destruction.

But we are talking to believers, *or to those who consider themselves believers.* Therefore, following what we have said it is evident —if we want to respect all the laws of Logic and the evidence provided by common sense— that neither Judaism nor Islam *have God.* More clearly stated, *they do not have any God* nor do they want to have one. Hence, claiming that *they have the same God as we do* is an evident lie. And preaching this to Christians as if it were an unassailable truth is a hoax, a veritable crime that will lead many confused souls to Hell.

---

[42]1 Jn 2: 22–23.

The conversion of the Jewish People, which will take place immediately before the Parousia, is a revealed *mystery* whose realization is
another *mystery* in itself, which God has kept to Himself. Given the
constant forcefulness of their rejection of Jesus Christ and their veritable blocking of the roads that lead to Him, this much is quite clear:
the conversion of the Jews will be the result of an *extraordinary* event
established by God from the Cross as a proof of His overflowing mercy
towards His chosen People; it will never be a consequence of *congratu-
lations, hugs, and friendly conversations* with the Catholic Hierarchy.
Believing otherwise is but the upshot of the foolishness and madness
of having abandoned the Faith.

Catholic theology and pastoral action have abandoned —or at least
have seemingly forgotten— the only *Way* that leads to Christian existence and fills it with meaning. One can easily verify that Jesus Christ
is not the central point of current Preaching in the Church; he needs
only to listen to the preaching on any Sunday in any church —not to
mention the themes that are dealt with by this preaching.

This abandonment is especially relevant when it comes to the issue
with which this essay is concerned. The books about mystic theology,
even those on the very treatises by the mystics, hardly adopt as a
reference point the crucial issue of the essential necessity of Jesus Christ
on the road that leads to union with God, as we will see later.

It is astounding, even shocking, therefore, to note the disregard for
fundamental texts of Revelation without which any attempt to erect
or explain Christian existence is doomed to collapse.

As we have said, Jesus Christ is the *central point* on
which the divine–human relationship of love hinges. Without Him, the part played by the human being in his relationship of love with God would be *practically non–*

existent. In effect, the soul learns how to love God through the Person of Jesus Christ, Whom she perceives in His divine-human Nature.

This relationship thus established, our Lord becomes the *thou* to whom the human *I* addresses himself, as equals and in complete intimacy, via a supernatural conversation that transcends any human reality. Nevertheless, we must emphasize that one cannot dispense with the *human* component of the structure of this relationship because the way the soul loves, even when elevated by grace to the supernatural order, must always follow the exigencies of her own nature (grace elevates, doesn't destroy, nature). As we will see later, Jesus Christ is of the essence here, for He is known by the human soul in His Human Nature with *logical priority.*

How to explain, nevertheless, the process of a conversation between fiery lovers when one of them is Jesus Christ? Evidently, we have reached the threshold —merely the threshold— of what is most intimate and difficult to analyze of the divine–human relationship of love.

In order to achieve some inside knowledge of the sentiments of the soul in her love relationship with Jesus Christ, which is lived and experienced mainly in the highest degrees of mystical prayer, one must first acquire certain knowledge of the sentiments of Jesus Christ towards that

soul. After all, this is a *relationship* of love whose essential
elements are reciprocity and bilaterality and whose initia-
tion —let us not forget this fact— has been taken by Jesus
Christ, for *He first hath loved us.*[43] Only then can we realize —although in a confused way which cannot be more
than a mere approximation— what happens at times in
this intimate relationship: the torrents of love that each
heart reciprocally exchanges with the other; the tenderness
and mystery of the words and compliments of love uttered
by the mouth of Jesus Christ and addressed to the soul;
the whispers of love that both lovers mutually interchange
and whose content and meaning —absolutely unintelligible to any third party alien to this relationship— stays
always with them; the caresses of love that each lover lav-
ishes on the other echoing the inspired poetry of the *Song
of Songs...*

And yet, we stumble upon the insoluble problem of
plumbing the intimate nature of the love of Jesus Christ
for the soul, despite the fact that Revelation speaks about
this love as it exists in the Heart of Jesus Christ: *You
may be able to comprehend, with all the saints, what is the
breadth and length and height and depth; and to know also*

---

[43] 1 Jn 4:19.

the charity of Christ, which surpasseth all knowledge.[44] We know that His love is real and immeasurable. Nevertheless, from the outside of this mystic relationship, only those souls who have fully answered the Love offered and given to them can gain an insight into the knowledge of what there is in that abyss.

The soul that realizes that she is the object of the love of Jesus Christ, true God and true Man, in this relationship of love that takes place in the intimacy of *I for thou–thou for me* feels herself inebriated and beside herself, to say the least. She could never have imagined that somebody could be loved in such a way; least of all loved by a Divine Lover Who deals with her on *equal terms* and Whose joy it is to appear as totally in love with her and smitten by her love.

Things being so, it would be a sight to see —should one be able to gaze at the mystic relationship from the outside— the feelings of the soul when she sees herself the object of this love, and at her attempts to offer it a suitable welcome; her loving words and compliments with which she tries to correspond to those of her Divine Lover; her daring intention of accepting the challenge of love to which He has called her...; all of which ends up in babbling,

---

[44]Eph 3: 18–19.

caresses, and sighs so loaded with trembling emotion as to plunge her into an out–of–herself experience —her heart beating in a way she never felt before—, in an impossible attempt, to the point of exhaustion, to show her own love to her Husband. It is here that wonder takes over again. In effect, given that her attempts finally show her deficiency, *God Himself* provides the soul with suitable sentiments and words: *Likewise, the Spirit also helpeth our infirmity. For we know not what we should pray for as we ought; but the Spirit himself asketh for us with unspeakable groanings.*[45]

Therefore, according to Saint Paul, once our inability to adequately talk with God takes hold, the Spirit then intervenes to ask for us with *unspeakable groanings*.

This text is usually wrongly interpreted as, given our helplessness, the Spirit *prays for us* with unspeakable groanings. This interpretation cannot be but erroneous because it is difficult to imagine the Spirit exhaling a *groan*. It seems more reasonable to understand that the Spirit provides us with ways of manifesting our sentiments that go beyond our possibilities; ways that are termed as *groans* because they must be given a name more in accordance with reality and more intelligible to man.

---

[45]Rom 8:26.

We must note here that, apart from taking the insufficiencies of human language into account, the word *groaning* does not always means a manifestation of sorrow; it can be also used to refer to highly exhilarating states of the soul caused by feelings of supreme joy.

In the higher moments of mystical prayer the soul is flooded with such unspeakable feelings derived from her intimate relationship with Jesus Christ that they are absolutely indescribable and inexpressible outside this loving relationship. So much so that the soul would not be able to withstand the intensity of these feelings without assistance from the Spirit. Which is only the indication that the Divine Lover belongs to an essentially higher order than the one corresponding to the human lover; for His love is human and divine at the same time: this unfathomable mystery effected by the hypostatic union enables the divine Person Who gives His love to a mere creature to give it as both *God* and *Man*.

Although I cannot go beyond the threshold when I try to scrutinize the mysteries of the divine–human relationship of love, I inevitably feel nostalgia when realizing the marvels that the Love of God grants some souls. They are indeed *chosen souls*, or that is what has always been said. But the truth is that nobody has explained if such souls have responded with a yes to God's Love because He has chosen them, or if maybe He has chosen them because they have welcomed the divine offering and have responded in return with full generosity. And because we will never know the reason, we do not want to risk knowing what would have happened to us if we had opened our hearts to God's call.

We are well aware that a generous answer to the Love of God entails a *risk*, but we have never had the courage to admit it; a dangerous risk, indeed, which we dared not face. That is why we got used to thinking that dangerous adventures and great deeds properly belong to totally exceptional men; we did not realize that they were exceptional men because they had the courage to carry out those exploits, and many of them lacked extraordinary qualities before they set out in pursuit of those risky ventures. Such is man; he thinks that not letting problems overwhelm him is a safe and comfortable way to avoid making life difficult for himself.

But I have always thought with nostalgia about the marvels of divine Love. Contemplating them from afar, of course —as when one guesses, rather than sees, the misty snow on high, difficult–to–climb mountains—, my imagination has always looked at them as the only existing *reality* in the midst of a world no more solid than a hazy dawn. Or perhaps I considered them a fantasy–like *dream* able to transform and elevate one's life which, at present, is filled with mediocrity and whose seemingly outstanding characteristic is that it is abundantly tedious and boring. This is the most serious issue of my own life. I have been constantly tormented by the contrast between its average content and the lofty and superabundant true Life: *I am come that they may have life and may have it more abundantly.*[46] However, as usual, and to follow a very general rule, I have always tried to avoid this idea. And as for the words of the Lord..., they have always seemed beautiful; but as beautiful things made to be seen or heard, nothing more.

But I owe God the grace of having realized both that love is the only thing that gives meaning to human existence and that love also

---

[46] Jn 10:10.

means *totality*. It has always been evident to me that it is impossible to combine concepts that do not fit together, as *love* and *proportionality*.

Maybe that is why I have never stopped feeling the need of a *thou* to whom I could open myself and offer my heart, as, at the same time, I felt requited by him with the gift of his heart. As one can well understand, I am talking about the need to love and be loved. Deep down, I am talking about the insatiable hunger for beauty, goodness, and truth. These are the essential elements that always go with love as precedencies; they can be offered to me, not by any human *thou* who can merely provide them in part, but rather only by the *Thou* Who fully contains them and Whose only desire is to give them to me in their full totality. In effect, even if beauty, goodness, and truth were *partly* donated to me, my soul would always harbor the unquenchable desire for the remainder of that *all* that was not there.

This is why my *I* always felt incomplete without that *Thou* Who could totally fill my heart but Whom I never had.

It must be well understood that I do not mean that my personal *I* needs a relationship with any *other* to be such *I*. It is evident that an *I* must first be integral and complete in himself before beginning any relationship with another. Otherwise, how could one give himself completely —the only way for love to exist— if he does not previously possess the plenitude of *complete personality*? In effect, one cannot give himself *totally* is he is not himself *complete* in his being.

I have always been aware that my earthly existence, like the existence of any man, is a *pilgrimage*: constantly walking on a road whose bends and obstacles to come are totally unknown as well as what is ahead before reaching the end. I have always had the certainty that some day the road will come to an end and that Somebody is waiting for me there. In the meantime I go on walking, trying to forget my weariness, searching the horizon for signs that may indicate the end of

the road is near and that the moment of the encounter which I have
waited for and ardently desired for such a long time has finally arrived.

> *And seeing the road's end on the horizon,*
> *Urged by great longings, so weary, yet I run*
> *To where the trail ends with its mist and shadows,*
> *Leaving behind all my labors and sad woes.*[47]

The soul gets to know the Human Nature of Jesus
Christ in a *first moment* of perception and as the object
to which she directly channels the torrent of her love. But
she also perceives in a *second moment* His Divine Nature,
through which she meets the Divine Person with Whom
she finally falls in love (for love is always a relationship
between persons). Note that we are speaking about logical
moments, not temporal, because the creature feels herself
united to her Lord in *one only and single act of love.*

This explains that the divine–human dialogue, within
the heights reached by contemplative and unitive prayer,
contains, as a single whole, an *absolutely divine* part to-

---

[47]Cfr. *CFC*, 2. In the Spanish original:

> *Y el final del camino divisado,*
> *yo corro, por el ansia apresurado,*
> *hasta donde se acaba la vereda*
> *y el duro trajinar atrás se queda.*

gether with another *perfectly human*; but these two parts can never be considered as distinct and separable elements.

In short, a set of elements that clearly shows the difficulty of this attempt: to understand the nature and progress of contemplative prayer. The divine element is the principal part of the divine–human relationship and, truly speaking, the determining factor and origin of all the obstacles presented by the complex and mysterious features of this issue —for those alien to these features who try to know them, as well as for the very soul that would like to explain them (to others or to herself). Some go so far as to say that, in this sense, the divine factor is a truly *disturbing* element.

Logically the soul is the subject most directly and principally affected by this *disturbance*.[48]

---

[48] Once again, as always, we stumble upon the limitations of language. In this essay I have tried to refrain, without much success despite my serious efforts, from using the expression *human soul*. In fact, the correct term is *man* or *human being* as the single–unit compound of body and soul and as the subject really affected by the mystical phenomena. Unfortunately, centuries–old practice has imposed the use of the concept *soul*, which is but the aftermath of distant and subconscious memories of Manichaeism and those trends of thought (within Platonic tradition) suspicious of the human body, in turn shared by some Fathers (the Pseudo–Dionysius, Saint Augustine), and even by some well–renowned mystics, as Saint John of the Cross.

At this moment, the conversation between the divine and human lovers, steeped as it is in divinity, becomes as highly *human* as the limitations of human nature allow.[49] At the same time, the conversation is also as *divine* as is allowed by the receptive capacity of infinitude that a created means may have, or as supported by a human nature that still is a *viator* in her pilgrimage toward her Homeland.

And we have reached the limit which cannot be transgressed, either from outside to inside or from inside to outside. No stranger to contemplative prayer can enter it, nor can the mystical soul overcome the obstacle that bars the way out and explain it.

Having delved as deep as is allowed to our meager means into the knowledge of what happens within the intimacy of the divine–human love relationship where one of the lovers is a divine Person, it is time to stop and explore other ways.

From now on we can only proceed by bits of knowledge which barely exceed the boundaries of mere conjecture.

---

[49]The human element of this dialogue elevates it to the highest level human nature can reach. Hence, this dialogue, despite remaining, in this regard, within the strict limits of what would be required by a rigorous quality of *humanity*, could not be understood by a human being incapable of overcoming the boundaries of a standard apogee.

We can refer to the personal testimony of mystics and the observation of those external phenomena that sometimes accompany contemplative prayer; the best known being *stigmata* (Saint Francis of Assisi and Padre Pio of Pietrelcina, among the most notable), *transverberation* (Saint Teresa of Jesus), *levitation, raptures,* and *ecstasies.* These phenomena are not contemplative prayer; they are merely external signs used by God to bear witness to the depths that the love between Him and His creature could reach.[50]

We are reaching towards what is totally ineffable, where the soul, having gone beyond the very limits of eternity, is about to lose all track and sense of time. *Perennity* being an essential element of perfect love, transcendence regarding the tracking of time is but a pledge or warranty of eternity where the reality of that love will take place. By the same token, the soul enjoys here a foretaste of that Perfect Joy;[51] therefore she momentarily loses the chains

---

[50]Testimony of something must not be mistaken for the thing itself. The very expression (*testimony of*) indicates that we are dealing with two different realities. Testimony is just an instrument to bring closer and confirm the authenticity of something or somebody; it provides a ray of light for those who cannot grasp the whole reality of the thing in question.

[51]Perfect Joy, to be perfect, needs the element of perennity (joy would not be perfect if you know that, in time, it is going to stop) which can only occur in the timeless time of Eternal Life.

that have tied her to time: *I love you before the existence
of time, I have loved you within time, and I will love you
beyond time...*; it is little wonder that the Letter to the Hebrews says: *Jesus Christ, yesterday, and today, and the
same forever.*[52]

Most noteworthy in deep contemplative prayer is the
painful torment that affects the soul at this stage of her
spiritual life. This kind of torment —whose intensity is
known only to God and the soul—, which is at the same
time suffering and joy, could very well be termed, so to
speak, as the highest degree of both sensations. One of the
mysteries of love is the possibility that the highest degree
of sorrow becomes equally and at the same time the highest intensity of joy for the soul. Perhaps the soul, seeing
herself pierced and mortally wounded by love, feels such a
great longing for being ever more and more immersed in
this love so as to cause in her a proportionally painful sentiment. More pain as she experiences more love; thus the
Letter to the Hebrews says that *our God is a consuming
fire.*[53]

One might fall into an error of perspective while walking along such strange, mysterious, and intricate paths

---

[52]Heb 13:8.
[53]Heb 12:29.

of love. It would happen if one puts too much emphasis on the greatness of God as Infinite Being, losing sight, in so doing, of the smallness His Love wanted to take upon Himself so that we could love Him perfectly; that is, according to our own way and manner as human beings. Indeed, there is always the possibility that what is infinitely large may hide what is extremely small. And yet, knowing the state of God as Husband and Friend of the soul is paramount to understanding His loving relationship with her.

This is where the bride, madly in love, breathes deep and painful sighs sprouting as cries from the depths of her soul. And since the bride has already been wounded by the Infinite Fire that is consuming her, she vehemently begs her Divine Spouse to make her hot coals and to not stop until she becomes only cinders. That is why the bride, as she is being consumed in this fire, desires to burn more and more until she finds herself struggling against an insoluble dilemma: on the one hand, she is disturbed because she does not know how resilient she will be as she faces this ceaseless stream of flames that are gradually turning her into fire; on the other, she thinks that the possibility that those flames may cease would be even more difficult to bear.

In the meantime, the Bridegroom continues giving His assaults of love to the bride, which she also most ardently desires in this tournament or combat of love to which both challenge each other. As recognized by the bride in the *Song* in this known passage:

> *He brought me to the banqueting house,*
> *And his banner over me was love.*[54]

The Bridegroom haunts her with His endearing words, passionate compliments, and fiery heartbreaking darts of love:

> *Arise, make haste, my love,*
> *My dove, my beautiful one, and come.*
> *For winter is now past,*
> *The rain is over and gone.*
>
> ....
>
> *My dove in the clefts of the rock,*
> *In the hollow places of the wall,*
> *Shew me thy face, let thy voice sound in my ears;*
> *For thy voice is sweet, and thy face comely.*[55]

---

[54] Sg 2:4.

[55] Sg 2: 10–11.14.

Note again that the poetry of the *Song of Songs* can be a real *trap* for the ill–advised, that is, those who do not reach beyond the superficiality of the letter of this Book, including those experts who only revel in the beauty of the verses and even try to delve into the possible meanings of their elusive metaphors. This always happens with any human poetry. However, the poetic and inspired words of the *Song* do tell the truth of what they contain, but not the whole truth, *since what they conceal is infinitely more than what they reveal*; at least in the earlier stages of courtship and to the extent permitted by the capacity of the reader.

If we continue with the theme of the progress of mystical life in contemplative prayer, perhaps we have already reached the opportunity to talk about one of the proper phenomena of the stages that lead up to its consummation.

The flames of love that consume the contemplative soul, like the burning bush contemplated by Moses, never burn out: *And the fire never saith: it is enough.*[56] Therefore, a moment must come when the bride, overwhelmed and exhausted by the weight of love, feels faint, as the bride of the *Song* expressly says:

---

[56]Prov 30:16.

> *Stay me up with flagons,*
> *Comfort me with apples;*
> *Because I languish with love.*[57]

With the fainting or *dying of love* that the soul experiences in herself, contemplative prayer is near its zenith. One could ask whether or not this so–called *mystical death* is real death. According to the testimonies we have, one must admit that this process can end in a real death caused by the impetus of love; this is what usually happens with the death of the saints.

Mystical death is a slow process in which the soul begins to experience symptoms of death because of love, as a foretaste of the possession of her Bridegroom in the Eternal Life that is waiting for her. Paradoxically, it is an abundance of life that she really experiences; actually, there is a gain or improvement of one's life as the Apostle says: *For to me, to live is Christ, and do die is gain.*[58]

At this point in contemplative prayer, the importance and splendor of material things fade away to usher in the flashes of beauty radiating from Jesus Christ. And the same thing happens to the soul with respect to the sounds of the world: the comings and goings of men, the suffering

---

[57]Sg 2:5.
[58]Phil 1:21.

of many and the joys of a few, death and life, laughter and tears, success and failure, justice and iniquity... and so many things in the world that try in earnest to be part of the personal existence of each man. All those things become more distant as if their sharp shapes were disappearing gradually into places where oblivion eventually gives way to nothingness. Even Nature and the infinite wonders that fill it sound to her as an increasingly muffled rumor: the summer nights with the twinkling throbbing of the stars; the whisper of the sunset wind in the woods of lost and forgotten valleys; the warm and rosy dawn in the immense prairies; the breeze that caresses the shores of blue and calm seas; the silence of the high snowy peaks, never defiled by human footprint; the wakes of ships plowing white curls into wide oceans of endless horizons; the cooing of the turtledove in the nearby stream, calling hidden in silent trees newly dressed by springtime... All are losing their reality in the presence of the Beloved when the mysterious silence and awaited solitude, in which the *thou* and the *I* of both lovers find themselves, now finally make possible the dialogue of love which is heard and understood only by them.

But Love is consuming the strength of the enamored soul. She is, after all, the same simple creature who one day, time ago, filled with profound astonishment and a flaming fire, found herself next to the Beloved, Who invited her to enter the banquet hall as He raised over her a banner challenging her to a tournament of love (Sg 2:4). Man, even aided by grace and all the other special gifts from God, cannot bear such a heavy weight in this life. Even more, nostalgia, longing, and desire to enjoy a Whole, Who is now only partly possessed but felt as increasingly closer, make him run with irresistible momentum there where he knows his heart has always been; where also the Bridegroom is waiting for him from before the beginning of Ages and prior to the establishment of all boundaries that limit Time. Thus, Saint John of the Cross echoed this very longing that urged the bride of the *Song*:

> *O shepherds, you that, yonder,*
> *Go through the sheepfolds of the slope on high,*
> *If you, as there you wander,*
> *Should chance my love to spy,*
> *Then tell him that I suffer, grieve, and die.*[59]

---

[59]Saint John of the Cross, *Spiritual Canticle*. Note that in the last verse there is an ascending progression of the three verbs: *suffer, grieve,* and *die.* Dámaso Alonso underlines their well–staved and distinctive nuances that the Saint himself mentions in his Commentaries. Dámaso Alosno, *Poesía Española*, Gredos, Madrid 1981, p. 294.

This longing is the only thing that gives meaning to this life. A human existence not lived in longing caused by enamored Hope and in yearning for union with Jesus Christ resembles a life which perhaps never reached its End because that life had no beginning either; poetry tries to put it this way:

> *If living is to love and to be loved so,*
> *My only longing is to live in Love's glow;*
> *If dying is of love to burn in ardor*
> *That consumes the heart, may I quickly die more.*[60]

---

[60] *CFC*, 90. In the Spanish original:

> *Si vivir es amar y ser amado,*
> *sólo anhelo vivir enamorado;*
> *si la muerte es de amor ardiente fuego*
> *que abrasa el corazón, muera yo luego.*

3. Conclusion

I said earlier that I intended to talk *about* contemplative prayer, emphasizing the preposition with the obvious intention of delineating the necessary limits of the subject. Still, at the end I realize that I have not even managed to go beyond the surface of this issue. As the mere amateur that I am on this subject, I can very well say in my defense that my only intention was the simple desire, nothing further, to write a few lines expressing my enthusiasm for and devotion to Saint Teresa of Avila, using *contemplative prayer* as a pretext: actually, a simple *amusement*, full of innocence and good intentions.

Nevertheless, it is dangerous to confront some issues: if one gets closer to the fire, he gets burned; this is exactly what happened to me.

I remember my younger years when, in some of my early works, I had the opportunity of referring to mental prayer as explained by Saint Teresa. As everyone knows, in order to show the difference between mere mental prayer and contemplation, the Saint uses her famous example of the various ways of getting water to differentiate one from the other. According to her, the work of the soul was essential to mental prayer: the water is drawn by hand

and with tiresome toil; or perhaps pulled out of the well with the help of the wheel. Whereas contemplative prayer, always according to the Saint, is comparable to what happens with the rain: water falls from the sky abundantly without requiring any effort on our part. She took this example to stress the *purely passive* attitude of the contemplative soul before God, to Whom she attributed *all activity* during contemplation.

I have always believed that the so–called *contemplative prayer* is the most perfect act of love that man is able to accomplish in this life. And since the act of love is the most perfect of all acts of the human soul, and since love necessarily is bilateral and mutual correspondence between the two lovers, it is very difficult to imagine that the human soul should only adopt at that moment a merely *passive* attitude before God; this mere passivity would seem to go against the nature of things. No lover takes a passive attitude in the presence of the beloved when their loving relationship reaches the highest degree of vital intensity and when emotions, mutual dialogue, and intimate sentiments are totally *common* to both lovers. As I understand this, neither God nor His creature can remain *passive* at the highest point of their relationship of love.

With the passing of years, I came to understand that things are not always as clear and as evident as we believe

them to be. This is why I now find that I am not surprised
that I was not able to understand Saint Teresa. After
all, she was a saint and a true mystic, well versed in the
intimate relationship of love with the Divine Bridegroom,
and a Doctor of the Church.

God was after me since I was a child, planting in my
heart a desire for holiness. The same God Whom I have
always willfully tried to avoid as if He had nothing to do
with me. Indeed, my preferences always leaned toward an
ordinary, uneventful life where the issue of true love was
never given a chance. Even now I am still doubtful of
having definitively abandoned this choice.

If it is true that *all is grace* as Bernanos said, *contemplative prayer* is a special grace from God that He grants
to whomever He wants. As in the case of holiness, it would
be serious impudence and temerity to insist on achieving
contemplative prayer on our own, through a nonsensical
search that would undoubtedly be condemned to failure.

But an ordinary and common life does not have to be
a sad and wretched one if it is accompanied by a trust
in God which is not willing to quit and by an attitude
that allows for the possibility of *against hope believing in
hope* (Rom 4:18). Keeping oneself firm in the midst of
darkness, not abandoning the road and overcoming fear,
maintaining the unyielding longing and hope of finding

something different undoubtedly implies great courage. If someone is able to do these things, it is because he hopes with enthusiasm in the possibility that some day, perhaps at the turn of an unexpected bend in the road, he may find a milestone indicating a different bearing.

And yet, I cannot help thinking that *contemplative prayer* is much more than a merely *passive* attitude on the part of the human soul. I do not even like that term to refer to prayer, for I think that it cannot express, even by far, the true content of prayer; despite the fact that Saint Teresa has followed here, as all classic mystics and masters of spirituality have done, the doctrine of Saint Thomas about beatific vision consisting in the *fulfilling contemplation of Truth.*

I am sure that both Saintly Doctors, despite my intemperance, are happy to spare the boldness of this inexperienced writer who stubbornly thinks that Perfect Joy, the ultimate end to which we are destined, besides being the *fulfilling contemplation of Truth* will also include the *contemplation of Infinite Beauty*, and, above all, the *Possession of Supreme Goodness.*

In the meantime, in the midst of successes and errors, victories and defeats, moments of darkness and lights of hope, my own and everyone else's life goes on, as does the Road to our Homeland. In the meantime, the sun will go on flooding with his light the cheerful spring mornings, the torrid days of summer, and —now timidly— even the gray autumn afternoons or colder winter sunsets. Meanwhile, the stars will continue with their stubborn intention of looking like lantern lights hung in the sky, providing a semblance of hope in the Dark of our lives.

And we will continue seeking the true meaning of *contemplative prayer*. It will be a laborious task that can urge us to try the roads leading to it, if we find them, or to abandon ourselves in the hands of a God Who loves us, should we not succeed in discovering them; always walking and scanning the horizon, eagerly awaiting the arrival of the Bridegroom. And we are confident that someday, at the most unexpected moment, we will find Him for Whom our soul has so much longed. And when this happens, we may well believe that we have just awakened in order to be escorted into the sweetest of dreams. At last, the end of a Time already passed will arrive, only to usher in the commencement of a Time without time. This will be the time to reminisce the old verses of ancient Songs; which, according to fables, sirens still sing during the nights of summer in the inaccessible beaches of unknown seas:

And there, when early spring had come once again
On the side of the mountain,
Almond trees now budding with flowers anew,
Shades of white, shimmering with fresh drops of dew,
Or soft, tender, beautiful rose–colored hue,
There weighed down with sorrow my wounded heart bled
Because You have left my love unrequited
While I contemplated your face earnestly...
At last I woke up to what enamored me,
Bathed in floods of tears I knew my grief was done
And a wonderful sweet dream had just begun.[61]

---

[61] *CFC*, 97. In the Spanish original:

Y, cuando al comenzar la primavera,
del monte en la ladera,
los almendros en brotes florecidos
en tonos blancos y tornasolados
o en suaves, tiernos y bellos sonrosados,
donde mi corazón sangraba herido
por haber Tú a mi amor correspondido
al par que yo tu rostro contemplaba...
Hasta que enamorado al fin me despertaba,
en torrentes de lágrimas bañado,
de un dulce sueño, apenas comenzado.

Second Part

Structure of
Mystical Prayer

1. Prolegomena

When I was still a student at the Seminary, I had the opportunity to meet a priest with a reputation for being a spiritual man with a deep inner life. He was in great demand to give all kinds of spiritual retreats, conferences, and meditations at novitiates, religious communities, seminars, etc.; he was even requested to lead the famous *Cursillos in Christianity*, which, at that time, began to be known and which he handled as a true expert.

Many years after my return from South America, I met with him briefly a few times. I sadly realized, however, that he had suffered a loss of mental powers that prevented him from behaving normally. He asserted that he had spent a long time in various countries and had made contact with some Eastern religions, apparently without committing to any of them. He seemed to be a very different person now that he was back and older, after probably having undergone not a few sufferings during his numerous trips back and forth (wild and aimless, as I understood). One day I heard that he was teaching some sort of a three–day workshop which he called a *Cursillo to learn how to practice contemplative prayer.* Obviously, this undertaking had no explanation other than the mental instability of my old friend, whom I always considered a good priest nonetheless.

As any one can understand, it is simply not possible to *learn* how to practice contemplative prayer, and, of course, never in three days; nor in a thousand years, not even if one were able to live one hundred thousand lives. Contemplative prayer is something essentially *supernatural* and a gratuitous gift from God that He grants to whomever and whenever He wants; therefore this prayer is owed to nobody, and nobody can merit it, for it belongs to a level so high that man's natural powers cannot reach.

I must admit that I am not sure of the reasons that prompted me to write about such a topic, for it is difficult and unknown to me, since I have never been granted any mystical experience. Maybe I was moved by one of those strange impulses that often spring from the heart and about which, as Pascal would say, the reason understands nothing.

But humans need to dream of things that are impossible to accomplish; and occasionally, we need to attempt them, for not all madness is evil.

Thanks to the madness of Don Quixote, for example, we could witness the birth of an immortal adventure. And I have often asked myself why there are so many who believe that the amazing Epic lived by our hidalgo Alonso Quijano ended in dismal failure. This topic, I think, could turn into a long debate that would probably lead us to quite unexpected as well as surprising conclusions. Many grand and good projects have been designed to meliorate the world, and a number of them have proved not to be successful, probably because of the world rather than the project itself. The Apostle Saint Paul, for example, spoke about the foolishness of preaching and about the stumbling block of the Cross; he insisted that there was no other way to Salvation. Since then, the only thing clear is that Christianity cannot be perceived as being totally deprived of folly, at least as folly is understood by the world.

The harsh realities of the world in which we live anguish us because of their patent coarseness and vulgarity. Not to mention the evil and lies that surround us everywhere, which often make us feel anxious and virtual victims of despair. And hence the question: Would it be wrong to try to combat such snares and such feelings by procedures that might bring us succor and surely some personal progress?

Undoubtedly, any attempt to talk about issues like contemplative prayer, when thick darkness is looming over the world and especially over the Church, cannot be but a crazy (some would say desperate) effort to confront a problem seemingly impossible to master. And yet, there are but two possible options: either look the other way and not think about what is happening, or face the facts and look Above precisely now that we can feel the Abyss of corruption trying to engulf us and force us to look downward. One can only choose the latter; and one has to be careful while walking, as do those who are climbing a high summit, to not look down and be overcome by a vertigo that would lead to death.

We common Christians know well that contemplative prayer is an inaccessible topic for us; consequently our knowledge about it is confined to what little we can understand of what the mystics tell us. Nevertheless, even this scanty cognizance reaches the deepest core of our soul, making us long for whatever we can intuit. It is as if we were before a new and wonderful city of Oz that can be seen at dawn through distant mist, adorned with the soft blue of her towers, and her crystalline buildings crowned by bright constellations as the rays of an invisible Sun enfold her with his mantle of bright light. This longing is one of the enterprises that men sometimes make the object of their daring; and even if they be doomed to failure, the remains salvaged from their shipwreck are amply sufficient to justify undertaking them.

2. About the doctrinal authority of the Spanish Mystics and the meaning of these Contributions

Note that when I speak here of *Spanish Mystics* I am referring exclusively to Saint John of the Cross and Saint Teresa of Jesus, whom I consider to be the zenith of the Mystical Literature of the Spanish Golden Age and the most outstanding mystics of the universal Christian Spirituality.

Also note that we are not going to question here the orthodoxy, doctrinal rectitude, or extraordinary heights of the doctrine of either Mystic.

The methodology that we will follow in this study is rather *a question of approaches and points of view in the expounding of the doctrines.*

Consequently, we will explain the following program:

Delving into the nature and development of contemplative prayer to find out if *certain points of their teachings,* written and expressed by these two Mystics, *are susceptible to some clarification.*

Considering the possibility that some aspects of their teachings —most notably in the case of Saint John of the Cross— may be expounded in a more *positive* way; or, better put, made more *accessible*. This does not indicate any intention to minimize the basic requirements that make up the basis of a true spiritual life and especially of mystical life.

The spirituality to be outlined here is *essentially the same* as that taught by Saint Teresa of Avila and Saint John of the Cross. Nevertheless, since some of their systematical explanations may seem difficult and burdensome —today they are often regarded as too demanding and even impossible except for extraordinary souls— to the mindset of modern man, we will address the task of trying to consider them in a more *accessible* and humane manner.

Note, and this is the last point in the exposition of the entire plan of this study, that we will also try to highlight and give due relevance to certain issues which, despite their importance, do not seem to have merited adequate attention from our two great Mystics.

3. Diverse approaches regarding the indispensability of the cross and purification in mystical prayer

When we speak of mystical prayer we are not necessarily referring to contemplative prayer, unless otherwise expressly stated, but rather to any more advanced prayer destined to lead the soul on the road to intimate union with God.

We will pay special attention to some *obscure*, or *seemingly austere*, points contained in the spirituality of our Mystics. The terrible *Nights of the senses* and *of the spirit* of Saint John of the Cross, for example, is a subject whose mere explanation and difficult reading can instill in many souls a fear of finding their way along the trails of mystical prayer. Therefore, it is a real challenge to try to truthfully *present* such doctrines to the man of today without altering their content. It is only a matter of making them appear more accessible and in alignment with the mentality of those who, today, want to approach them.

This could perhaps lead to the false impression that we intend to offer here a spirituality that ignores the Cross and the need for personal repentance and penance regarding personal sins; nothing is further from our thoughts.

The spiritualities that cancel out the Cross and try to extinguish in man the sense of sin, as is intended, for example, by the theories of *anonymous Christianity* and *universal salvation*, are expressions of the modernist heresy that currently pervades the Church. The intrinsic perversion of those teachings is easily detectable because they *nullify and destroy the very notion of love.*[62]

Thus we can make way for the elucidation of the importance of the Cross in Christian life and its implications vis–à–vis the doctrine of the Spanish Mystics.

After man, because of original sin, lost the state of original justice in which he had been created, he was restored back into fellowship with God through the Redemption carried out by Jesus Christ; this is called *objective Redemption.* But this Redemption, in order to be effective, needs man's free and full cooperation in taking advantage of it (*subjective Redemption*), which is accomplished through repentance of sins and works proper to Christian existence performed with the help of grace.[63]

Thus, man makes his own the Redemption obtained by Christ by living a Christian life with all its labors, by his sufferings and in doing penance for his sins, even by his

---

[62]I study this topic in detail in several of my works.

[63]Modernism totally fails to consider subjective Redemption.

own death accepted as punishment for sin and ultimate instrument of reparation; all this carried out for the love of Christ, with Christ, and in union with Christ.

But the love of God for man, materialized and made real in the Person of Jesus Christ, goes far beyond that. In effect, from now on man's sufferings and death have the *new value of sharing in those of Jesus Christ*; therefore, the life and death of a Christian are equated to the life and death of Jesus Christ, with all the value that such a thing entails. *For none of us liveth to himself, and no man dieth to himself. For whether we live, we live unto the Lord; or whether we die, we die unto the Lord. Therefore, whether we live or whether we die, we are the Lord's.*[64]

This is how Saint Paul states the fundamental principle which constitutes the final and definitive purpose of Christian existence: *Know you not that all we who are baptized in Christ Jesus are baptized in his death?*[65]

In turn, this participation in Christ's death —which is the reason for our baptism—[66] has a dual purpose that provides a twofold result:

---

[64]Rom 14: 7–8.

[65]Rom 6:3.

[66]Modernism has never taken this essential truth into consideration either.

First, Christian Dogma considers as a fundamental value the participation in the sufferings and death of the Lord by every human being as a means of his personal redemption and as the instrument that opens the door to Salvation.

Second, such participation is also a *response* to the infinite Love shown by Jesus Christ in the Redemption and which is now accessible to every man. According to this purpose, very commonly forgotten by the Doctrine, the soul would be willing to suffer with Christ out of pure love only, willingly sharing His death even if such a thing *were not necessary for her own salvation.* Now the soul seeks above all to share the existence of the Beloved, both in life and in death. For her, the desire for her own salvation would no longer be as pressing as the longing to share *everything* with the beloved —Jesus Christ, in this case— as required by the rules of perfect love.

Consequently, man's participation in the sufferings and death of Christ opens for him a new and exciting horizon: the ability to delve deeper, to an extent quite unknown, into the mysterious and bottomless depths of Love; an endless chasm which would be ready, like the open pit of a newly discovered diamond mine, to be explored and exploited by those who believe that they have a heart possessed by the divine touch of insatiability.

This dual aspect, which considers the possibility of sharing in the sufferings and death of Jesus Christ, is probably that which is *least highlighted* in the works of the Spanish Mystics. Of course, the presence of these dual *realities* in the doctrine of our Mystics cannot be doubted since this dual aspect is part of the mystery of Christian life. But there is the distinct possibility that its importance as a valuable element of mystical prayer has gone *unnoticed* in the development of their spiritual doctrine. To which the fact should be added that some aspects of Saint John's doctrine are difficult to assimilate and may need a special explanation, which probably will not be easy.

Although this is not the place to study the impact of sin on human nature —which, strictly speaking, is a theological issue—, let us recall that after the fall human nature was *scarred* and subject to far–reaching consequences.

God Himself intervened through the Person of the Word, and the element of *guilt* that sin had left imprinted on man was entirely eliminated by Redemption. Therefore, human nature reached the state of being *repaired.* However, the incidence of sin left on the soul an imprint deep enough for *sorrow* to be part of all earthly existence.[67] It is well understood that the condition of being subject to suffering and pain

---

[67]It is the consequence of what has been called by theologians the *debt of punishment,* as far as man's being subject to sorrow during his earthly existence is concerned. Another thing altogether is the purging condition of the souls in Purgatory, and, of course, the eternal suffering of the damned in Hell.

embraces all men, including those who had nothing to do with sin, as Jesus Christ (true Man, after all) and the Virgin Mary who was freed from sin by grace.

There is a twofold reason for this encompassing universality of sorrow. First, because Jesus Christ accomplished Redemption through His death on the Cross, thus fulfilling the will of the Father which He assumed voluntarily. And second because it was the Father's benevolent determination, also endorsed by Jesus Christ, that man should cooperate in this redemptive Reparation with his own suffering and death through his voluntary choice to assume them.

As can be easily deduced from what has been said, the *ultimate* reason for the painful fate human nature has to endure throughout this earthly existence is nothing other than *love*; without removing the distinctive nature of suffering as a punishment for man, love transcends and surpasses this nature, thus giving it a new condition. And here is where Jesus Christ comes in as a determining factor. The fact that man cooperates in atoning for his fault, through his participation in the sufferings and death of Christ, is not as important as the opportunity of joining his Lord through such suffering *because of love*. Indeed, as the Doctrine teaches, not even the death of Jesus Christ would have been necessary to effect man's Redemption.

Both Saint Teresa and Saint John of the Cross center their doctrine in the absolute necessity of the *purification of the soul* to reach, through it, *her ascension to God.*

In the doctrine of Saint Teresa, the soul passes through the mazes and intricacies of the Mansions of the *Interior Castle.* The Saint shows the various modes of purification and detachment from created things, which are necessary to advance in the ways of mystical and even contemplative prayer and whose purpose is simply union with God. Her spirituality, otherwise so sublime and elevated, seems to be more accessible and feasible than that of Saint John of the Cross.

The paths of prayer taught by the Saint Poet of Fontiveros can cause anxiety in unprepared persons. In addition to the abandonment of all created things, the Saint requires the *absolute negation* of all the senses, both internal and external, and even the powers of the soul. According to his doctrine, such detachment of the soul from all material and spiritual things, among which is also the idea of the Humanity of Jesus Christ, is necessary to complete the arduous *Ascent of Mount Carmel* and achieve pure contemplation of the infinite God that transcends all matter and any created thing.[68]

On the other hand, our two Spanish Mystics *do not directly propound* the various methods of sharing the sufferings and death of Christ, as we have explained them.

Here we will consider a different perspective. As we have said, and always with a view to the exercise and de-

---

[68]It is difficult not to see here the influence of late Platonism, always persistent in Christianity, tenaciously mistrustful of matter, particularly of the human body, which, Saint Augustine assures us, is the prison of the soul.

velopment of mystical and contemplative prayer —or at least to the ways leading to them—, we will try to explain a more accessible and ostensibly more positive form of spirituality. Accordingly, this spirituality will be based on the poetic and expressive metaphors that describe the amorous mystical relationship between the divine Husband and His bride –God and man's soul— contained in the inspired Book the *Song of Songs.*

Ultimately, this study aims to offer a number of possible approaches to the *same immemorial reality*, which is none other than the mystical Christian Spirituality, although here viewed from different angles and making special mention of some important aspects of doctrine that may have been less emphasized by our Mystics. Additionally, a particular reference will be made to certain points more difficult to understand, especially in the writings of Saint John of the Cross.

4. Contemplative prayer from the point of view of the *Song of Songs* and mystic poetry. Necessary antecedents

The perfect love of God for man expects to be requited by an equally perfect love of man for God. For God would not want to love and be loved in any other way. As for man, and always according to his abilities, it would not be fair if his response to the love received were not also *total*.

This is nothing more than the fundamental law of love which is the total personal offering of the lover who expects to be requited, in turn, with the absolutely total love of the beloved.

The Bride of the *Song* expresses very clearly the total and mutual possession by the two lovers. The pronouncement in the first verse of Song 6:3, *I am my beloved's, and my beloved is mine*, is quite surprising and unexpected in a poetic Book of the Old Testament, for it involves the most glaring admission of the possession of a soul by God and of the *possession of God by the soul*. Such affirmation of this incredible and *reciprocal* love is like a foretaste of the full Revelation of the Love of God given, in turn, to man already capable of responding, which normally should not have been accomplished until the arrival of the New Covenant:

> *I am my beloved's, and my beloved is mine:*
> *He feedeth among the lilies.*[69]

---

[69]Sg 6:3; cf 2:6; 7:11.

This is the expression of true love because it is true love: *I belong to my beloved and my beloved belongs to me.* God takes Logic very seriously; therefore, for Him things are what they are. However, total Truth overwhelms man to the point of vertigo. Consequently, he can handle only small slices of Logic: delayed self–surrender, partial and conditional love, adulterated and diminished truth because it would be compromising if accepted in its entirety, etc.: *And the light shineth in darkness; and the darkness did not comprehend it.*[70]

Unfortunately, this mutual and reciprocal belonging, notwithstanding its being an essential element of love, usually goes unnoticed in treatises dealing with the divine–human relationship of love. Indeed, they always speak of union with God, the purification necessary to attain it, the states of mystical exaltation typical of the higher degrees of prayer which lead to contemplation of God, etc.; but they always seem to be missing all reference to a relationship of *mutual correspondence.* And yet, the notion of *relationship* indicates a uniting element that connects at least two people.

It follows that when those treatises explore the origin and expansion of contemplative prayer they also neglect

---

[70] Jn 1:5.

another important aspect: the soul feels a burning desire to undergo the same sufferings and death of Christ. It is true that such an important reality is always dealt with, at least implicitly, in the doctrines which study contemplative prayer; nevertheless, a more complete and *explicit* expounding of this principle that has important consequences for mystical prayer is always welcome. The desire of the soul for necessary purification, on which both writers and mystics themselves insist, and which can be considered as highly reasonable, usually does not exceed her desire to *personally undergo the same destiny as her beloved*:

> *If only in my walking through the valley*
> *By the fir tree forest I could meet with you,*
> *And could contemplate you finally anew,*
> *Death from love I would share with you completely...!*[71]

The desire to possess completely the beloved person and to become, in turn, the beloved's complete possession

---

[71] *CFC*, 27. In the Spanish original:

> *¡Si al recorrer el valle yo pudiera*
> *en el bosque de abetos encontrarte,*
> *para que, al fin, de nuevo al contemplarte*
> *muerte de amor contigo compartiera...!*

is a corollary of the longing that each lover feels for sharing the destiny of the other in a plenitude that includes the yearning for partaking in the better and the worse, joy and sorrow, happiness and suffering: *Rejoice with them that rejoice; weep with them that weep.*[72]

The reciprocal *thou* and *I*, explicit or implicit, an inseparable element of the relationship of love and of the intimate union of both lovers, is not usually overlooked in mystical poetry. Saint John of the Cross beautifully expresses this reality through his descriptions of the intimacy of the relationship of love between the Bridegroom and the bride, but not in a direct way. The bride has entered the *long–aspired garden*, and now she rests, *her neck leant*, in the arms of the Beloved:

> *Now, as she long aspired,*
> *Into the garden comes the bride, a guest:*
> *And in its shade retired*
> *Has leant her neck to rest*
> *Against the gentle arm of the Desired.*[73]

When speaking about prayer, one cannot dispense with the deep sentiments that the soul experiences in her inti-

---

[72]Rom 12:15.

[73]Saint John of the Cross, *Spiritual Canticle.*

mate conversation with Jesus Christ which result in ineffable joy. This is one of the incentives that impels her to search and long for an intimate relationship in which she ends up being crushed, overwhelmed by sentiments that result not so much in words but rather a throbbing heart caused by her nearness to the Bridegroom. But He also shares in the thrill of their being together. And both desire that this mutual company they are enjoying may last for an unending time:

> *My Beloved compelled me*
> *To forget my cares and worries and sorrow,*
> *And fly to his side only,*
> *While the Sun grants his bright rays to us below*
> *And the Moon illumines the night with her glow.*[74]

Once again, mystic poetry tries to sing in its own way the mystery of the divine–human love relationship. Its literary metaphors bring into play the beauty of nature,

---

[74] *CFC*, 34, 61. In the Spanish original:

> *Me requirió el Amado*
> *para que de las cosas me olvidara,*
> *y fuérame a su lado*
> *mientras que el Sol sus rayos otorgara*
> *y a la noche la Luna iluminara.*

thus making reference to the perfume of the flowers, the enticing charm of evening suppers, or the mysterious energy of love which *moves the sun and the other stars*, as the Divine Poet put it:

> *Beloved, I am longing*
> *To taste your supper in the fresh garden air;*
> *For once again it is spring*
> *And sweet, fresh breezes are fair*
> *With the perfumes of sage and mint that grow there.*[75]
>
> *My Love, our climb goes steeply*
> *To hills with rosemary–rockrose covering,*
> *Where we two will drink deeply*
> *From the pure abundant spring*
> *And taste waters fresh and clear and murmuring.*[76]

---

[75] *CFC*, 47. In the Spanish original:

> *Amado, yo quisiera*
> *al aire del jardín gustar tu cena,*
> *pues es la primavera*
> *y el monte ya se llena*
> *de romero, tomillo y hierbabuena.*

[76] *CFC*, 49. In the Spanish original:

> *Mi amado, subiremos*
> *al monte del tomillo y de la jara,*
> *y luego beberemos*
> *los dos, en la alfaguara,*
> *el agua rumorosa, fresca y clara.*

It is regrettable that some forms of prayer —valid and absolutely necessary— such as prayer of supplication and prayer expressing sorrow and repentance before God may make one forget about the existence of other loftier kinds, the various types of mystical prayer.

Nor is sorrow, as a determining motivation for love, given due attention in the treatises dealing with prayer. However, the power of suffering as the driving force behind love is stronger than the power derived from joy. The beloved person is seen with joy when he is happy; but undoubtedly he is the object of greater love when he is the subject of suffering. This is not surprising when one considers that sorrow is the heritage of this Earth (which some call a *Valley of Tears*), while joy is rather a condition belonging to Heaven.

It may seem extraordinary and contradictory, but the fact is that the sorrow whose ultimate determining motive is love is never an occasion for merely sadness but rather, and above all, for joy. We must not forget that man is a pilgrim in a strange country where sorrow is the easiest item to find but which, contrary to what many might think, is at the same time an extraordinary source of beatitude: *Blessed are those who mourn, for they shall be comforted.* Rarely has anyone come to realize that calling those who mourn blessed is one of the (apparently) greatest inconsistencies ever uttered by any human tongue; hence the grandeur of the audacity to proclaim it.

Sorrow is for the soul the truest, most guaranteed path that will lead her to the Divine Spouse. Any Christian, merely by being a Christian, is destined to walk the steep path leading to life (Mt 7:14). Nevertheless, there is no doubt that the Christian, after having traveled the difficult roads of his existence, will finally hear one day the call of the Bridegroom. And the same will occur —let us not abandon our subject— to him who dares to try to overcome the difficult initial moments of prayer. Both will have to fight against a world always ready to persecute those who want to live according to Christ (2 Tim 3:12). Fortunately, as the Christian's participation in the sufferings of Christ becomes more intense, the greater also will be his love and the more abundant the fruit yielded (Jn 12:24).

In the end, after the soul has accomplished her many labors and overcomes the trials caused by the absence of God, she will hear the greatly desired voice of the Bridegroom. A voice that will kindly echo the difficult ways she had to tread so laboriously and which will beckon her to come to Him from wherever she is: whether in the crags of the mountains, in the dens of wild beasts, or in unknown caverns; and the voice will take her to the joyful prayer of union. Poetic metaphors used by the holy Book are truly beautiful and the descriptions that refer to the diverse byways and various difficulties that the soul has had to overcome in order to behold the arrival of this moment are exquisite:

> *Come from Libanus, my spouse,*
> *Come from Libanus, come;*
> *Thou shalt be crowned from the top of Amana,*
> *From the top of Sanir and Hermon,*
> *From the dens of the lions,*
> *From the mountains of the leopards...*[77]

Christians do not always take sufficiently into account that Jesus Christ, by finally overcoming sin and death, brought a final end to the disastrous consequences that they once had upon man. Hence, *the meaning of death and suffering has changed* because of Jesus Christ, and in the only way the infinite wisdom of God is able to imagine. Since then sorrow has become a principle capable of

---

[77]Sg 4:8.

raising the degree of divine–human love to inconceivable intensity.[78]

The *Redemption* effected by Jesus Christ brought about the elevation of human nature from the state of *fallen* nature, because of sin, to the state of nature *repaired* and reconciled with God. With Redemption the doors of Salvation were opened to all men, provided that they were willing to achieve it through their required personal cooperation.

At the heart of Jesus Christ, and always in compliance with His Father's designs, was the desire to *make our sins His own.* Not in the sense of making our Redemption more effective and secure or attributing to Himself the consequences of our guilt, but out of obedience to a feeling sprung from the depths of love: *to suffer with us.* Or put another way, the desire to *feel in His flesh our own suffering;* which is but the result of a love so large that it is unable to stand seeing us suffer without making our

---

[78]It is true that some blessed souls living on this Earth, thanks to their deep love for Jesus Christ, have shared in an extraordinary way the sufferings of His passion and death; consequently they were granted such special mystical graces as transverberation or the stigmata. But the fact that the souls that have enjoyed these singular phenomena are so few demonstrates the paltry regard that the Sufferings and Death of Christ have earned in the practice of mystical prayer.

sufferings His own. This means that He wanted to suffer not only *for* us but also *with* us.

Thus the way to the possibility of contemplative prayer was open, which is the substance and summit of this study. And now the divine–human relationship of love, once the Incarnation of the Word became a reality, is possible thanks only to the *Human Nature of Jesus Christ*; hence our line of thought considers this the central point of this essay.

For our part, we are convinced that if our Mystics had put greater emphasis on the Human Nature of Jesus Christ they would have made their doctrines on divine–human relations more understandable, as well as more flexible and *human*, specifically their teaching regarding the possibility of and advancement in mystical prayer. This is why we take as our starting point the behavior in the purely human love relationship, as does the *Song of Songs*. Thus it becomes possible to portray the divine–human relationship with expressive and intelligible terms similar to those used to describe the way merely human love operates, such as a mutual search on the part of both Bridegroom and bride; their jousting and tournaments in their relationship of love; tender and affectionate terms in their mutual rapport; their reciprocal longings because of their absences; their waiting, each one for the other; etc.

Indeed, the human soul cannot love Jesus Christ to a degree of rapture required by perfect love *if she does not love Him as man and as God.* Her love for Jesus Christ *begins* with her perception, through faith, of His Human Nature, *followed* by that of His Divine Nature; and ultimately, through the latter, the perception of His divine Person. And it is not possible to find any other path that leads *directly* to the love of God, for *no man cometh to the Father, but by me*;[79] otherwise it would be quite difficult to understand why the Son of God became Man.

We must not forget, of course, that the soul loves the Person of Jesus Christ *in one and unique act of loving*, in which the succession of the two perceptions just alluded to is purely logical and not temporal, as has already been sufficiently explained in the First Part of this study.

The soul loves Jesus Christ *in a human manner*, but elevated by grace, while the Person of Jesus Christ loves her, with a single act of love, in a *divine as well as human way.* This is possible thanks to the *Hypostatic Union*, an expression which denotes the mystery of the one divine Person of Jesus Christ possessing two Natures.

Thanks to this, and through the various stages of development of mystical prayer, *the soul increasingly loves*

---

[79] Jn 14:6.

Jesus Christ while feeling herself increasingly loved by Him.
This feeling, as we have just suggested, does not affect the
creature exclusively; like everything that happens in love
and according to the known law of reciprocity, it must be
equally attributed to Jesus Christ (in His divine as well as
in His human way of loving). Without it mystical prayer,
and in general the entire development of the divine–human
relationship of love, would be unthinkable. Later we will
mention the Christological doctrine of the *Communication of Idioms*, which is another mystery whose nature
and comprehension are the backbone of the doctrine about
mystical prayer set forth here.

So the whole scheme of the divine–human relationship
of love is laid out: Jesus Christ loves the human soul as
True God and as *Perfect Man*. It is a *divine–human* love,
reciprocally requited by the human soul with a human love
that has become *human–divine*.[80] If what we have said so
far is true, one can concede the difficulty in understanding
the doctrine of Saint John of the Cross concerning the need
to dispense with the Humanity of Jesus Christ once the
highest degree of prayer has been attained.

---

[80]The human soul will always love in a human way even if elevated
by grace, for each being acts according to his nature, whether elevated
or not.

If these considerations are accepted then the task of explaining the nature of the divine–human relationship of love is facilitated. To this purpose we will adopt a point of view that shows the convenience of using the sacred book *Song of Songs* as *leitmotif*. Therefore, we will consider what is essential to the human relationship of love as materialized in the conjugal love and union as the *Song* also does. This makes it seem a more human and approachable Spirituality which, without losing a bit of the depth and truth of its contents, may open new horizons so that the paths of mystical prayer are seen as less difficult.

We should not forget throughout this study that bilaterality and reciprocity are always essential conditions for love; both are emphasized here with particular importance, for this essay would not be possible without their consideration. Classical mystical doctrines *do not normally stress* the opportunity or the need for these two key elements, particularly the works of Saint John of the Cross. Here, on the contrary, the entire exposition of the divine–human relationship of love hinges on them.

And since it is assumed in this study that the soul falls in love with God *in the Person of Jesus Christ*, we should bring to mind, if only briefly and in relation to the doctrine of the Hypostatic Union and the dual nature —Divine and Human— of Jesus Christ, the doctrine of *Communication of Idioms* in Christological theology. It may not be necessary to recall that both Natures, properly belonging to the divine Person of Jesus Christ, form one whole perfect union, but without any kind of admixture.

By the Hypostatic Union in Christ of His two Natures, the doctrine known as *Communication of Idioms* allows one to attribute to the Divine Person of Jesus Christ specifically human characteristics insofar as they do not involve defects incompatible with His Divinity. For example, there are situations in which Jesus Christ (and we assume that He has no intention of pretending) asks questions in trying to understand what is going on around him or what someone's wishes are; or where He is not paying attention to the surrounding reality (as in the dangerous occurrence of a storm in the middle of the lake, when He had to be awakened by His disciples). There are other times when He is affected by feelings of joy, sadness, or pain, and even of anger, etc. All this must be taken into account if one wants to understand the way in which the divine–human relationship of love behaves.

5. The divine–human relationship of love throughout our way of attaining contemplative prayer

After what has been said above, we are better prepared to reflect on the divine–human relationship of love.

It seems logical to start focusing our attention on the first degrees and initial moments of mystical prayer; those in which the soul begins to feel the first amorous emotions caused by God and the ensuing discovery of the superiority of divine love over human love.

The falling in love of two persons usually takes place progressively. It starts with an initial moment of mutual knowledge which is ordinarily followed by a process in which each person is smitten with love for the other.

At this point one can appreciate the similarities between divine–human love and merely human love which can be used as descriptive elements. The *Song of Songs* follows this procedure as it gradually describes the divine–human relationship of love on a peculiar stage whose actors are God and the creature. Any other interpretation of the main object of this sacred Book renders the following exposition useless.

God always takes the initiative (1 Jn 4:19) and begins to slowly seduce the soul in a process which cannot exclude a reciprocal response from the soul in accord with the known rules of love.

The process through which the soul falls in love with God *in Jesus Christ* was effectively explained in the First Part of this essay. Thus it is easy to understand that the central point of this explanation is to try to establish a parallelism between the divine–human relationship of love and contemplative prayer at its outset and during its development.

If the divine–human relationship of love, which we are going to describe now, is to have any *real* and not merely imaginary meaning then one must admit that God acts in this relationship by giving *pride of place* to the intervention of the Human Nature of Jesus Christ. As we all know, He Who loves is always the divine Person of Jesus (love is possible only between persons) Who at times (let us recall the doctrine of *Communication of Idioms*) acts through His Human Nature (for example, His death on the Cross) that now takes place in a special foreground. The human soul, which always loves in a human way, although now divinized, needs to perceive the *presence* of the Humanity of Jesus Christ as a *priority* in her relationship of love with Him. However, we must insist on saying that she loves with only one act of love, by which the soul welcomes Him as God and as Man.

In the *Song*, the Bridegroom begins by explaining how He fell in love with the bride:

> *Thou hast wounded my heart, my sister, my spouse,*
> *Thou hast wounded my heart with one of thy eyes,*
> *And with one hair of thy neck.*[81]

This first meeting with the Lord deeply affects the soul and marks her indelibly for life. She feels wounded with love and almost beside herself because she has discovered, for the first time in her life, a kind of love totally unknown to her.

Nevertheless, the same occurrences that mark all events of human life will be present here. For God does not allow the soul that loves Him and has taken the true path to reach Him to think that she has discovered a way to happiness in which there are no setbacks or obstacles. The soul who decides to venture into mystical prayer, whose object is none other than union with God, must take into account that there will be many situations in her journey where she will experience an abundance of mixed feelings: moments of joy mixed with others of sorrow; moments of light alternating with darkness; and also present will be the anxiety produced by the absence of the Lord and the resulting anguish.

---

[81]Sg 4:9.

The soul cannot be surprised at something that could happen at any time: that God hides and even seems to have abandoned her completely.

> *As you passed you gazed at me*
> *With that silent insinuation love keeps,*
> *Then you left me suddenly*
> *Searching in the hills and deeps*
> *Among the rocks and steep cliffs where the stag leaps.*[82]

We have often stressed that poetry can express better than prose those events that most profoundly affect the human heart, which are the immediate cause of many diverse reactions and varied forms of response. Again the inadequacy of human language makes itself felt: words always fail to encompass the meaning of concepts; and concepts never have sufficient power to reflect the feelings of the soul. Saint John of the Cross echoes this in one of his most beautiful stanzas:

---

[82] *CFC*, 102. In the Spanish original:

> *Al paso me miraste*
> *en silenciosa insinuación de amores,*
> *y luego me dejaste*
> *buscando en los alcores*
> *en los riscos de gamos saltadores.*

> *Where can you hiding be,*
> *Beloved, that you left me thus to moan*
> *While like the stag you flee*
> *Leaving the wound with me?*
> *I followed calling loud, but you had flown.*[83]

A first period of enthusiasm, whose indeterminate duration always depends on the decisions of Divine Wisdom, is followed by a period of possible disappointments in which the soul is in danger of despairing. Surely the designs of God allow this situation so that the soul may learn that she will not enjoy the delights of divine love if she does not first experience the Cross of her Savior. Hence only the souls endowed with a sufficient spirit of fortitude are able to embark on these roads and then follow them. This is precisely why there are so few souls that persevere in, let alone complete, this endeavor.

Normally, souls who have a noble heart, though suffering the absence of the Beloved, are not willing to give up easily, for it would mean losing the great chance of starting on the path of holiness, the only purpose for which man has been created; an opportunity which most likely will not be offered again, as the saying attributed to Saint Augustine goes: *Fear the Lord passing by for He might not return.*

---

[83]Saint John of the Cross, *Spiritual Canticle.*

One proof of true love is that it is always determined to be faithful in adversity, patient in the midst of sorrow, and never giving in to discouragement. The enamored soul will never abandon her passionate search in the certainty that she will end up finding her Beloved:

> *I now live in darkness bleak*
> *Nostalgia's pain holds me bound*
> *And from love so wounded weak*
> *I die... you I have not found.*[84]

> *Have you heard my moans and tears...?*
> *May my weeping, as I grieve,*
> *Borne on sighs of winds that breathe,*
> *Bring my sorrow to your ears...!*[85]

As one may guess, human mystic poetry only follows in the footsteps of the poems of the *Song of Songs*. Both ex-

---

[84]In the Spanish original:

> *En la oscuridad he vivido*
> *de nostalgia alimentado,*
> *y tan de amores herido,*
> *que muero, pues no te he hallado.*

[85] *CFC*, 103. In the Spanish original:

> *¿Oíste al fin mis gemidos...?*
> *¡Si acaso el triste lamento*
> *llevara en alas del viento*
> *mi llanto hasta tus oídos...!*

press the same sentiment of longing and sorrow caused by the absence of the Bridegroom; but they soon realize that those sufferings, as if by paradox, actually are the skeleton key to true joy, the precious fruit that comes directly from the Holy Spirit.

But we should not deviate from the *leitmotif* of the *Song of Songs* —lest somebody may think that we are establishing our own teaching; let us then listen to the laments of the bride in the very words of the sacred Book. Indeed, its poetry could seem at times sharp and stark, but we must not forget that we are dealing with a translation of ancient manuscripts written in an also extremely old language by a People whose philosophy and ways of expression are totally different from ours. And yet, one can easily grasp the greatness and beauty of a poetry which, ultimately, comes from Above:

> *I arose up to open to my beloved;*
> *My hands dropped with myrrh,*
> *And my fingers were full of the choicest myrrh.*
> *I opened the bolt of my door to my beloved;*
> *But he had turned aside, and was gone.*
> *My soul melted when he spoke;*
> *I sought him, and found him not;*
> *I called, and he did not answer me.*[86]

---

[86] Sg 5: 5–6.

The search, usually long, has begun which tests the mettle of souls which have set out on their life of prayer. At first, the road seems long and difficult, but, as the poet says, it is the fortunate *yearning search of an enamored soul*:

> *O bitter trail so toilsome, you take great toll;*
> *You are wearying, rocky, rugged, and steep,*
> *Dangerous, hazardous, fraught with perils deep*
> *In the longing search of this enamored soul...![87]*

Therefore, it is not an ordinary search. Finding the beloved person is not a task similar to discovering a common treasure because the object being sought is the *greatest of them all*, in exchange of which nothing in existence can be considered its equal:

> *If a man should give all the substance of his house for love,*
> *He shall despise it as nothing.[88]*

---

[87] *CFC*, 92. In the Spanish original:

> *¡Oh amarga senda, dura y empinada,*
> *larga y abrupta, de aridez rocosa,*
> *que convirtió mi vida en azarosa*
> *búsqueda ansiosa de alma enamorada!*

[88] Sg 8:7.

The soul who with yearning desire tries to find her Lord through prayer, despite her sorrow in not having found Him yet, feels her heart overflowing with the joy of her search. As happens with the thirsty man who, walking in the desert, senses water nearby, the possibility of meeting Jesus increases the soul's longing and joy because of her very near and greatly anticipated encounter. God is not without compassion for those many poor souls who, loaded with the weight of their sins and their many faults still unmended, consider themselves sufficiently paid *if they are just allowed to look for Him.* Because, in the end, *every one that asketh, receiveth; and he that seeketh, findeth; and to him that knocketh, it shall be opened.*[89] And if God is able to take the form of a humble pilgrim who knocks at the door begging to be opened,

> *Open to me, my sister, my love,*
> *My dove, my undefiled.*
> *For my head is full of dew*
> *And my locks of the drops of the night,*[90]

the souls that know they are too small are content, for that very reason, with a longing for the *crumbs that fall from*

---

[89] Mt 7:8; Lk 11:10.

[90] Sg 5: 2–3.

their master's table (Mt 15:27). Contemplative prayer, high degrees of union with God, an intimate loving relationship between the Bridegroom and the bride...But perhaps these numerous souls —have we not sometimes felt tears of joy flowing down our cheeks when we realized that we were among them?—, like the blind man at Jericho, dare only attempt to *follow him in the way* (Mk 10:52), although from afar; just this makes them happy.

One of the great mysteries of the spiritual life is that the longing search for God, as sorrowful and painful as it may seem, becomes a source of wonderful joy for the soul because it is totally animated by love. On the contrary, all human endeavors to seek happiness in the things of this world will always be stamped with an expiration date, not to mention their inherent inability to fill the heart, as crass reality soon confirms.

It is normal that the soul, during her passionate search for God along the byways that crisscross the paths of mystical prayer, may often feel disoriented and almost on the verge of despair. But in the end she always sees a light that leads to other paths more favorable and passable, where the mere feeling of the closeness of the Bridegroom makes sorrow impossible:

> *I arrived at a crossroads along my way*
> *Without knowing where my life's destiny lay,*
> *And when the black veil of night fell around me*
> *I found myself lost in grief and misery.*
> *But vast numbers of stars crossed over the sky.*
> *And I saw myself with them as they passed by.*[91]

The darkness that sometimes surrounds the search begun by the soul is never so intense as to become blackness; not even during the terrible *Nights* (of the *senses* and of the *spirit*) described by Saint John of the Cross does the soul feel herself so abandoned by God as to fall into despair. The sorrowful anguish of the *Nights*, however hard it may seem, never fails to be accompanied by the mysterious *feeling* of the presence of the Spirit; and joy, as we know, is precisely one of His fruits (Gal 5:22).[92]

---

[91] *CFC*, 91. In the Spanish original:

> *Llegué a una encrucijada del camino*
> *sin saber de mi vida su destino,*
> *y al caer de la noche el negro velo*
> *perdido me encontré y en desconsuelo.*
> *Mas cruzó por el cielo un haz de estrellas*
> *y vi que yo formaba parte de ellas.*

[92] Mystical Spirituality would distinguish between sentiments of darkness and the nights, or between sentiments of despair and sentiments of hopelessness, depending on their origin being in God or in the Evil spirit, with totally opposite consequences.

But the dark moments or conditions of the soul during the *Nights* are transitional periods; they cannot be constant and continuous, otherwise they would render the divine–human relationship of love impossible. The logical thing would be, it seems, that the loving relationship would follow its normal course in which the lovers meet and get acquainted, talk to each other, mutually contemplate each other, and frequently exchange declarations of love.

All this takes place, of course, through the veil of faith. Saint Teresa speaks of the diverse phases in her perception of the presence of the Bridegroom, distinguishing what she calls imaginary visions (through the imagination, but real) from the intellectual ones.

On the contrary, Saint John of the Cross, who on this point is much more radical than Saint Teresa, inflexibly affirms that such visions or locutions *must be always and in every instance rejected* without any distinction, whether they seem to have originated from God or have indeed been caused by God. The Saint, always according to his teaching, bases his exigencies not so much on the need for preventing the danger of possible deception from the devil as on the obstacles to achieving a perfect union with God by the soul that these phenomena can cause. In order to accomplish this union, the soul must be entirely free from all things, good as well as bad, material as well as spiritual.

On this issue, we feel closer to the doctrine of Saint Teresa. Nevertheless, it must be taken into account that the mystical phenomena that exceed what is usually considered as normal (visions, locutions, or revelations) should never be desired or sought for their own sake, otherwise one would make way for the deceptions of the devil.[93] The best practice, therefore, is to let things take their course, with no other desire than to please God and to love Him with increasing intensity and to place oneself confidently in His hands. One must also not forget that one needs to be always obedient to the instructions and advice of a serious and competent spiritual director and never to be guided by one's own judgment or accept without discretion one's own guidance.

Saint Teresa also speaks about the conversations she held with Our Lord (locutions), distinguishing again between *imaginary* and *intellectual* locutions and giving us criteria to discern the authentic ones from those originating in the imagination of one's own soul. According to the Saint, one cannot but recognize the authentic divine locutions because the Lord Himself provides the soul with enough evidence.

---

[93]Humility is an exceptionally important virtue against which Satan uses all his cunningness to ensnare us. When the soul, for example, begins to believe that she is making progress along the path of humility, she can be sure that she is treading along the road to perdition.

The soul should take this point into account when praying; that is, the possibility of mistaking what seems to come from the Lord for what is but a product of her own imagination. If it is the first, then Our Lord's sayings *have in themselves the unambiguous note of authenticity that God Himself is giving them.* This is a peculiar situation which, as one can easily imagine, generally occurs to souls advanced in the mystical life. Nevertheless, when there is a lack of evidence or the slightest doubt about the authenticity of the sayings, it is better for the soul to attribute them to her own imagination, or not to pay too much attention to them, as Saint John of the Cross would say.

This does not mean in the least that the soul should be quick to reject them as false, for it is quite normal that God should inspire in man thoughts and good will through the use of his imagination. In reality, all the inspirations received by the soul for her own good come from the Holy Spirit. *Wherefore, I give you to understand that no man, speaking by the Spirit of God, saith Anathema to Jesus. And no man can say Lord Jesus, but by the Holy Ghost.*[94] If one ignores this reality, then the development of mystical

---

[94] 1 Cor 12:3. The criteria to discern the origin, either from a good or a bad spirit, of these inspirations are easy to apply. One has only to see if the effects produced in the soul are good or bad.

life as described here becomes impossible. The soul needs only to remember how difficult practicing true humility is, and how subtle the insinuations of the devil usually are.[95]

Once difficult times are over, the Bridegroom Himself, moved by the imperative necessity of love, insistently calls for His bride. For, as we have said repeatedly, the longings for meeting the beloved are greater in God than in His creature.

In trying to explain the early stages of the spiritual life of the soul, we can give way to our dreams —not exempt from reality—, and let them fly and imagine that the harsh winter has already covered the villages and the fields with a mantle of snow, that the rains have flooded roads and inundated meadows, and that the cold has forced people to hurriedly seek refuge in their homes. Then, when everything is over, the call of the Bridegroom for the bride takes place:

---

[95] True humility, as any other authentic virtue, is usually unknown to the humble person. Merely one's belief that he possesses this virtue is sufficient evidence to assert with full certainty that he is lacking it.

> *Arise, make haste, my love,*
> *My dove, my beautiful one, and come.*
> *For winter is now past,*
> *The rain is over and gone...*[96]

Now that *everything is past* —winter, cold, rains—, it is time to listen to the call of the Bridegroom.

Undoubtedly, suffering will have intensified the yearnings of the enamored soul for her meeting with Him, and perseverance itself will be the proof of the authenticity of her love. It is not that the Bridegroom requires any evidence to know about the love of the bride and whether it has attained enough maturity to make her self–giving effective. The evidence of true love is necessary, indeed, for the bride: the evidence of love obtained by going through the crucible of fire that are the sufferings and works lived in Christ, which are but the florilegium of Christian virtues.

The ultimate reason for this process will have to be found in the consequences of the original fall. After it, only the seal of suffering can authenticate the reality of love in the creature. Suffering alone, borne for the sake of the beloved, *for the joy of knowing that it is suffering because of the beloved and for the beloved,* is the authentic proof of love. The soul in love with Jesus Christ will necessarily feel impelled to suffer and die with Him, *and nothing else.*

---

[96]Sg 2: 10–11.

The common denominator of all this is that *each one of the two lovers ardently desires to share the life of the other*. In effect, the soul in love with Jesus Christ does not take into consideration or weigh up the difficulties of her sufferings according to their degree of intensity; *she accepts and wants those sufferings because they are the same as those of her Master and Lord*, Whom she believes to be the only meaning of her existence. In this way, love (the first fruit of the Holy Spirit) is the impulse that gives rise to the sufferings in Christ; and joy (the second fruit of the Holy Spirit) is what makes those sufferings not only bearable but also desirable.

This is the secret reason for the soul in love with God to suffer with joy, always finding meaning in the trials and difficulties of this life. Whereas he who does not love God has to suffer all the same, but without any motivation for his existence except that which despair can provide.[97]

---

[97]Eternal loneliness of self is one of the sufferings of the damned in Hell; and he will never find anybody with whom to share his despair. Nobody will ever listen to him, or understand him, or share his torments. The damned will not even pity himself, for all the positive qualities that naturally derive from the I (such as any possibility of compassion) will have disappeared. Even the possibility of relationship with another, which is the necessary origin of love, will have been lost forever.

Once winter, cold, and rains are past, the soul is finally capable of hearing the voice of the Bridegroom. Light follows darkness; day comes after night, and calm replaces the storm. Silence is broken by the sweet sound of the Bridegroom's voice, as the call of a bugle in the distance. The moment of forgetting the past and taking flight has come:

> *In your orchard a small bird,*
> *In grief at your absence, sang with a sad sound;*
> *And, when your soft voice she heard,*
> *Quickly rose up from the ground,*
> *To search in her swift flight where you could be found.*[98]

The soul is thrilled upon hearing the voice of the Bridegroom. Perhaps it was heard only in her imagination, but this did not impede the call from echoing within the depths of her being as if it were actually His call. Be that as it

---

[98] *CFC*, 9. In the Spanish original:

> *De tu vergel un ave*
> *por tu ausencia cantaba en desconsuelo;*
> *y oyó tu voz suave*
> *y, alzándose del suelo,*
> *a buscarte emprendió veloz su vuelo.*

may, it matters little if perchance the Bridegroom, even though He may not have arrived yet, has instilled this excitement in the heart of the bride as a preview of His meeting with her. Or maybe it has really been the voice of the Bridegroom, and then the bright rays of Heaven seem to be scattered all over the Earth. In either case, the soul feels the irrepressible momentum of her heart urging her to sing to the joy that the words of the Beloved cause in her.

> *Your sweet words of love to me*
> *Are coverlets weaved with soft threads in tandem*
> *On fields where flowers blow free.*
> *Come to my side, whisper them,*
> *Here in my garden of rosebud and linden.*[99]

It is impossible to think that the soul does not hear the voice of the Bridegroom during mystical prayer. The

---

[99] *CFC*, 53. In the Spanish original:

> *Son tus dichos de amores*
> *como una tela de suaves hilos*
> *en un lecho de flores.*
> *Ven a mi lado, y dilos,*
> *en mi jardín de rosas y de tilos.*

explanation of the method and manner in which this is done is irrelevant; and probably even impossible. What is sure is the *ardent desire of the Bridegroom to see the bride and hear her voice,* which necessarily implies the absolute necessity of the dialogue of love:

> *Come, my dove*
> *Hiding in the clefts of the rock,*
> *In the hollow places of the wall,*
> *Shew me thy face, let thy voice sound in my ears;*
> *For thy voice is sweet, and thy face comely.*[100]

And the heart of the bride, in turn, cannot help perceiving the voice of the Bridegroom, even beyond the hazy vigils of her sleep:

> *I sleep, and my heart watcheth:*
> *The voice of my beloved knocking.*[101]

Many are those who have allowed their lives to pass by without ever being conscious that God *had fallen in love with them.* There are also many who never imagined

---

[100]Sg 2: 13–14.
[101]Sg 5:2.

that they had the opportunity of *falling in love with God.*
The Enemy of God and Man has been clever enough to
spread the belief that mystical prayer is something only
for the mysteriously selected and chosen few. Even a great
number of consecrated souls think the same thing; victims
of an engulfing deceit, they never pause to think that there
is, indeed, a selection and that God is mainly responsible
for it, *but also that, in the last analysis, it is man who
effectively determines that selection through his free and
voluntary cooperation.*

What can a soul know about what could happen should
she have the courage to respond with generosity to the love
of God? Actually nothing. God alone knows how far an
Infinite Love can go Who is offered and freely and gener-
ously requited by His creature with his total capacity of
loving: *The spirit breatheth where he will and thou hear-
est his voice; but thou knowest not whence he cometh and
whither he goeth* (Jn 3:8). Nobody has been hampered
in terms of his power to surrender his life out of love, for
Jesus Christ spoke to all who would listen without adding
restrictions or imposing any discrimination: *He that shall
lose his life for me, shall find it* (Mt 10:39). But there is
something that can be held as definitively certain: whosoever does not respond to His call will not go anywhere.

An important point to be considered, which is a decisive element for mystical prayer to be possible and to grow, is the damaging skepticism of many souls who, afraid of being deceived by the devil or by their own imagination, never dare to fully trust in the love of God or run freely along the paths leading to the intimacy of the divine–human relationship of love. It would be essential for them to throw away, once and for all, the obstacles that, as fearful misgivings, impede them from believing in the reality of a *God Who has fallen in love with them*, and Who, therefore, wants to deal with them as true lovers do: in the intimacy of a love that is truly *human* and *divine* at the same time —the human–divine love that takes place between Jesus Christ and the soul, where Our Lord shows Himself and loves as God and as Man. It would suffice for those souls to let God lead them by the hand and to think and want nothing except to love Him and fulfill His will. Nevertheless, these souls must be sufficiently careful (but not obsessed) not to fall victim to excessive credulity while they keep vigilance about the importance of the virtue of humility. For the tendency to consider oneself a privileged soul depositary of special gifts of God *would be the worst idea that the devil could instill in the unfortunate soul willing to believe him.*

One has to admire the humble and simple question posed by the Blessed Virgin after the announcement of the Angel: *How shall this be done, because I know not man?* [102] She is ingenuously trying to learn the solution to an apparently impossible quandary, without giving any consideration to the dignity that results from her becoming the mother of the Son of God.

In any case, here, as in any relationship of love in which there are always a series of events and growth, the soul

---

[102]Lk 1:34.

needs to hear from the mouth of her Beloved that He loves her. Is it possible to conceive a true relationship of love in any different way? Man cannot love except in a human way (although supernaturalized by grace); hence we can ask ourselves what possible reasons could there be for depriving his relationship of love with God —a divine–human relationship— of its *human way* while it remains, nevertheless, a loving relationship:[103]

> *At my Love's side I lingered,*
> *In the silence of Love's mutual sweet word,*
> *While still at his side I heard*
> *Soft in my ear he whispered*
> *That he too, wounded by my love, has suffered.*[104]

---

[103] As for the manner of attaining this, without having to resort to the help of extraordinary phenomena, we must consider that one cannot put any hindrance to God, Whose ways of communicating with the soul are many, and Who has absolutely no need of giving explanations.

[104] *CFC*, n. 55. In the Spanish original:

> *Allí, junto al Amado,*
> *en silencioso amor correspondido,*
> *estando yo a su lado,*
> *Él musitó a mi oído*
> *que también por mi amor andaba herido.*

We are at the highest point of the divine–human relationship of love. The words of love that the soul perceives in prayer from the mouth of Jesus Christ Himself are able to cause in her a veritable rending of her heart and an intense sensation of being beside herself. In effect, the words pronounced by Him Who is *consuming fire*[105] cannot but cause this consequence. So extraordinary is the joy brought about in the soul that she may even believe that she is outside time after having forgotten, at last, all things:

> *Lost to myself I stayed*
> *My face upon my lover having laid*
> *From all endeavor ceasing:*
> *All my cares releasing*
> *Threw them amongst the lilies there to fade.*[106]

No wonder that in these circumstances the soul, trembling and consumed with excitement, begs the Lord to mitigate His enamored words lest she die out of love:

---

[105]Heb 12:29.

[106]Saint John of the Cross, *Dark Night*.

If you should see me again,
Down in the glen where the singing blackbirds fly,
Do not say you love me then
For, were You ever to repeat that sweet sigh,
On hearing it, I may die.[107]

The mystery of love within the divine–human relationship embodied, in turn, in mystical prayer is ineffable.

Thus, it is regrettable that the Spartan seriousness and the dryness of the treatise on prayer, as well as the tremendous demands for detachment and total annihilation, including the faculties of the soul, that derive from the doctrine of Saint John of the Cross,[108] induce in many people an erroneous apprehension toward prayer life, causing them to believe that prayer is an element of Christian

---

[107] *CFC*, 52. In the Spanish original:

Si de nuevo me vieres
allá en el valle, donde canta el mirlo,
no digas que me quieres,
no muera yo al oírlo
si acaso Tú volvieras a decirlo.

[108] Saint John of the Cross is an eminent Doctor of the Church, and, in our opinion, the Prince of the Christian Mystics. I insist that the clarifications made in this study with respect to certain points of his work do not mean a rejection of those points, but rather a mere verification that they are based on views that differ from our approach.

life for only a few individuals. In this way, the majority of Christians are forever excluded from the possibility of tasting the wonderful fruit from the garden where *myrrh and aromatical spices are gathered, and honeycomb and honey are eaten,* as the Bridegroom assures us.[109]

And the words of the two lovers are followed by their mutual gaze of love. The soul perceives Jesus Christ in this life through the light of faith only. But this light is more than enough to instill in her the sentiment that the loving gaze of the Beloved is an indispensable element in their mutual relationship of love. God Himself acknowledges it when He declares His love for the bride:

> *Thou hast wounded my heart, my sister, my spouse,*
> *Thou hast wounded my heart with one of thy eyes,*
> *And with one hair of thy neck.*[110]

There are indescribable alternating gazes, from the Bridegroom to the bride and from the bride to the Bridegroom; and it would be difficult to distinguish who is looking at whom because both are animated by the one and same heart:

---

[109]Sg 5:1.
[110]Sg 4:9.

Your look is tender, it is the dawn's own light,
It enchants the sun itself with great delight.
Your tears are morning dew that glisten and shine,
They hold the sweet intoxication of wine.
And when your eyes find mine and rest on them so,
The tears from my eyes become rivers that flow;
You cause wounds so deep with soft stares of your eyes,
That he upon whom you gaze out of love dies.[111]

One of the essential elements of any relationship of love, whether human or divine–human is *reciprocity*; therefore, it is also an important factor of mystical prayer that must be taken into account.

Accordingly, the desire and longing of the bride to find the Bridegroom are requited by the even greater yearning and desire of the Bridegroom to meet with the bride.

The Bridegroom, in His search, even knocks at the door in His burning desire to find the bride: *Behold, I*

---

[111] *CFC*, 76. In the Spanish original:

Es tierno tu mirar, luz de la aurora,
que al mismo sol seduce y enamora;
tu llanto es un rocío matutino
que induce a la embriaguez de un dulce vino.
Y al descansar tus ojos en los míos,
mis lágrimas semejan anchos ríos.
Pues tu suave mirar, tan hondo hiere,
que aquél en quien se posa, de amor muere.

stand at the gate, and knock. If any man shall hear my
voice, and open to me the door...[112] Or, as the *Song of
Songs* declares, the Bridegroom also resorts to a call whose
imploring aspect evidences His desires to be together with
the bride:

> *Open to me, my sister, my love,*
> *My dove, my undefiled;*
> *For my head is full of dew,*
> *And my locks of the drops of the night.*[113]

It is interesting to note that reciprocity in the divine–
human relationship of love is one of the most neglected
elements in the writings of mystics and spiritual authors.

Frequently God is portrayed as an Infinite Being Who
deserves to be worshiped and contemplated, but not as a
Being Who loves and has fixed His eyes on the beloved
person. In this way, God is a Being loved, but not a lover.
He usually appears as a seducing God, but not as one
seduced; as a listener, but not as one who talks; as one
with ears attentive to all sorts of amorous remarks or petitions, but not as someone who in turn utters them to

---

[112]Rev 3:20.
[113]Sg 5:2.

the beloved person with fiery words of love; as Lord, but not as a friend; as he who is able to move the heart of the enamored soul to the point of tears, but not as he who can equally shed them for the beloved person...

Mystical theology seems afraid to venture against the excellence of the Godhead. Consequently, the God of the Old Testament enjoys some primacy while the Mystery of the Incarnation is relegated to backstage. In this Spirituality, human nature is still under the influence of Platonism and its suspicions against the body; hence *apophatic* theology predominates over *cataphatic* theology. The echo of Saint Augustine's voice is still heard: *If you understand it, it is not God*; at the same time the unquestionable fact that the Word became Man in Jesus Christ is forgotten: *No man hath seen God at any time: the only begotten Son who is in the bosom of the Father, he hath declared him.*[114]

The justifiable zeal of mystical theology in maintaining the transcendence of the Godhead regarding every created thing affects another principle fundamental to any relationship of love, including, therefore, the divine–human relationship of love. We referred to this principle before as the *equalization* of levels between the two lovers, which

---

[114]Jn 1:18.

must be understood correctly in order to grasp everything involved in the possibility and progress of prayer.

The existence and progress of mystical prayer are based on the intimacy that follows the *person–to–person* of the divine–human relationship of love. This indispensable element does not pose any problem at all, given the nature of the relationship of love which demands necessarily that each lover —divine and human— *keep his own identity at all times.* On the other hand, as we have already said above, the soul's love of God is realized in the Person of Jesus Christ, towards Whom the soul directs all the affections of her heart in *one act* in which she apprehends Him at one and the same time as True God and Perfect Man.

The texts absolutely support this doctrine if we are referring to God's *humbling* Himself out of love in the Person of Jesus Christ. Saint Paul confidently exhorted the faithful at Philippi: *Let this mind be in you, which was also in Christ Jesus. Who being in the form of God, thought it not robbery to be equal with God, but emptied himself, taking the form of a servant, being made in the likeness of men, and in habit found as a man. He humbled himself, becoming obedient unto death, even to the death of the cross.*[115] And Jesus Christ Himself confided this astonish-

---

[115]Phil 2: 5–8.

ing declaration to His disciples: *I will not now call you servants: for the servant knoweth not what his lord doth. But I have called you friends: because all things whatsoever I have heard of my Father, I have made known to you.*[116] He also clearly affirmed the mission which within the setting of an extraordinarily humble life He came to this earth to attain: *For the Son of man also is not come to be ministered unto, but to minister, and to give his life as redemption for many.*[117]

The possibility of any kind of prayer is based on this, for there can be no relationship of love without total reciprocity. It is seemingly unthinkable to imagine that one party of that relationship would always talk while the other would always listen; that one party would contemplate and the other would always be contemplated; that one party would always be doing the asking without ever expecting any response from the other. This behavior would be alien to any kind of relationship; it would be a mere monologue that would not make any sense in a relationship of love.

The declaration of the bride in the *Song of Songs* (2:4) is extremely important. It contains two themes which de-

---

[116] Jn 15:15.

[117] Mk 10:45.

pend on each other but with each having a totally different nuance: the *banqueting house*, or the place where the wedding of the Bridegroom and the bride is going to take place, is one of them; the *contest of love*, which will take effect there and in which each lover will confront the other in the most singular of all imaginable contests, is the other theme. We will consider them separately:

> *He brought me to the banqueting house,*
> *And his banner over me is love.*[118]

According to the bride, she has been brought to the *banqueting* house undoubtedly because the Bridegroom's intention is to celebrate their wedding at the same time as they vie in a veritable joust or tournament of love.

As for the place of the celebration —*the banquet hall*—, if we take careful notice that this contest of love is going to take effect in a place typically used for banquets and merry-making, even seemingly coinciding with nuptial celebrations, we can have a fairly good idea of what the Bridegroom intends for His bride.

The circumstance of a *feast* to be celebrated gives rise in the human mind as to what is in store for the atten-

---

[118]Sg 2:4.

dants: fancy viands and delicacies, select wines in abundance, music and festive atmosphere everywhere, and things similarly appropriate for the occasion. And yet, these elements belong to a merely human *feast*, no matter how sumptuous man may imagine it; truly speaking, this banquet has little or nothing to do with genuine divine banquets, for the latter are celebrated within an entirely other and essentially superior order.

When we pass from the natural to the supernatural order, any attempt to describe the latter using human words and concepts is doomed to failure from the outset, notwithstanding the penchant of Modernist theology for not only moving easily from one order to the other but also dispensing with the supernatural order altogether.

Therefore, we must deal with this issue by elaborating some disquisitions that can somehow *approximate* us — here the implication of some sort of nearness would not seem appropriate— to the divine-human relationship of love that by now has reached its highest degree of intimacy. The unavoidable need to use human language compels us to acknowledge the inherent limitations of modest outlines of blurry and weak analogies which will tell us very little about the real content of this relationship but which will suffice to lead us toward a sweet sentiment of longing and joy.

At this point, only poetry could *bring us closer* to the notion of what a busy day of joyful festivity, pastoral in this case, would be; of course, within the limitations inherent to the difficult attempt to elevate one's mind from a purely human milieu to an entirely divine one.

> *The lights that morning was already pouring*
> *Brought life back to the green, shadowy valley,*
> *And one can hear, in the gorges, the soothing*
> *Strumming that combines soft rhythmic melody*
> *Like quaint guitars and rebecs*
> *And droning murmurs of cicada insects.*[119]

Mystical prayer must be considered an abundant feast. In this banquet, it makes no difference whether the soul comes into the presence of the Lord in the fervent joy of the intimacy of love or if she is called to share with Him the hardship of His cross. But there is no doubt that, in either case, it is for her a time of Perfect Joy.

---

[119] *CFC*, 31. In the Spanish original:

> *Las luces que la aurora derramaba*
> *la vida al verde valle devolvían,*
> *y abajo en la cañada se escuchaba*
> *el melodioso son, que al par hacían,*
> *rabeles y guitarras*
> *y el áspero runrún de las cigarras.*

The bride is joyful because she is finally with her Bridegroom after perceiving that He was coming closer to her:

> *My Lover came beside me*
> *As the morning sun rose over the hill crest,*
> *He gazed at me lovingly,*
> *And in his eyes I could see*
> *That one thing which only a kiss can cure best.*[120]

Saint John of the Cross expresses in his typically beautiful way the definitive repose of love once it has reached its summit and perfect joy. The Saint speaks of the *pleasant garden* referring to the *banquet house* that the bride mentions in the *Song of Songs*:

---

[120] *CFC*, 41. In the Spanish original:

> *Vino hasta mí el Amado*
> *cuando el sol se asomaba por el teso,*
> *y, habiéndome mirado,*
> *sentí en sus ojos eso*
> *que sólo amor lo sana con un beso.*

> *The bride has entered*
> *The pleasant and desirable garden,*
> *And there reposes to her heart's content;*
> *Her neck reclining*
> *On the sweet arms of the Beloved.*[121]

The soul no longer belongs to herself; she is totally her divine Bridegroom's, for nothing else is the end of Christian existence, the purpose of man's creation. This means that the soul has made hers the life of Christ and has put her life into the hands of her Bridegroom and Lord, thus fulfilling the sentence encapsulating the fundamental law of love:

My beloved is mine, and I am his.[122]

Behold the great secret of man's existence: discovering that *it is a more blessed thing to give, rather than to receive.*[123] For no other reason is *Gift* the most appropriate name given to the Holy Ghost and used since ancient times by the Fathers; this name expresses most clearly the

---

[121]Saint John of the Cross, *Spiritual Canticle.*

[122]Sg 2:16.

[123]Act 20:35.

essence of the Trinity: the eternal, mutual, and reciprocal *Donation* or self–giving of Love between the Father and the Son.

The soul that has made progress along the paths of prayer has attained a state in which she does not think so much of receiving as of loving God, once she has realized that Perfect Joy is nothing other than a *total self–giving to her heart's Beloved.* This is why there is a close relationship between true poverty and love, for the soul understands without a doubt that everything she is and has belongs to Jesus Christ, and that nothing is hers: *For none of us liveth to himself; and no man dieth to himself. For whether we live, we live unto the Lord; or whether we die, we die unto the Lord. Therefore, whether we live, or whether we die, we are the Lord's.*[124]

True prayer has nothing in common with any routine daily act of worship which has no apparent purpose other than to contribute somehow to one's own eternal salvation. Constancy in one's conversation and intercourse with Our Lord, authenticated by good works, infallibly leads to Joy which exists only in a place where are heard, along with seeing and possessing the Bridegroom, ancient and eternal songs known to lovers alone.

---

[124]Rom 14: 7–8.

> *To the high peaks capped with snow*
> *In vast whiteness of the mountains we ascend*
> *Moving through valleys, clearing chasms below,*
> *And there, at last, in the end,*
> *We can sing sweet love songs as our voices blend.*[125]

Every story is a true story in that it has an end. There is no *Neverending Story* of the renowned and beautiful fantasy of Michael Ende.[126] An eternal return to the beginning would be absurd and would make no sense for any rational creature; a road without end would lead nowhere.

Therefore, a moment will arrive when the soul, after the long and difficult journey of a life filled with labors suffered out of love and spent searching in earnest for God also through prayer —a time of indeterminate duration known to God alone— will see the end of her labors and

---

[125] *CFC*, 43. In the Spanish original:

> *A las nevadas cimas*
> *de las altas montañas subiremos*
> *cruzando abismos y salvando simas.*
> *Y, cuando al fin lleguemos,*
> *los cantos del amor entonaremos.*

[126] Michael Ende, *Die unendiiche Geschichte*, 1979. The English version was first published in 1983. Numerous versions in other languages followed.

the consummation of her existence. This means for her the possession of the Bridegroom, now in a perfect and never–ending love.

Now the soul recognizes her Bridegroom not only as Creator and Beginning of everything but also as her final End to Whom she has been destined and Who is now already reached and attained: *I am Alpha and Omega, the first and the last, the beginning and the end.*[127]

Sufferings, anxieties, uncertainties, and toils are gone, forever left behind:

> *If then together we follow the pathway,*
> *Let me precede you, arriving first, I pray,*
> *And there at the end of the road we will find,*
> *Our toils and hard labors are left far behind.*[128]

---

[127]Rev 22:13. Consequently, the story of the reprobate in Hell —to the extent that it makes any sense to call it a story— has no end, for he has forever lost the End for which he was born and to which he was destined.

[128]*CFC*, 2. In the Spanish original:

> *Si pues andamos juntos el sendero,*
> *deja que me adelante yo el primero*
> *allí donde se acaba la vereda*
> *y el duro trajinar atrás se queda.*

We referred to the distinctive *ludic nature* of the divine–human relationship of love when we discussed the declaration of the bride that she had been brought to the banquet house to contend with the Bridegroom in a *contest of love.*

The relationship between *games* and *contests* also called *jousts and tournaments* is well attested from time immemorial. The first Olympic competitions were called *Games* by the Greeks; the Romans used the same term to refer to those events celebrated in the Amphitheater or Circus. The latter, nevertheless, contained an element of cruelty, sometimes extreme, in the gladiatorial combats. There also was a fight to the death in the tournaments of the Medieval Period between competing knights, but only on special occasions and under much more humane conditions.

It follows from this that the elements of *game* and *contest* have always been linked. Yet we must add that the feature of *amusement* was part and parcel of both from ancient times and, therefore, was always present in competitions. It was not uncommon that the aspect of entertainment would remain as an exclusive attraction for the spectators, as always happened in the Roman amphitheaters where death matches were quite frequent.

The divine–human relationship transcends but does not exclude the character of *amusement*; in effect, it contains elements of sheer *game* (especially in its initial and simpler moments) and traits which are analogous to a *contest* (which generally appears in more advanced and subsequent degrees). At any rate, both aspects, game and contest, are present in any relationship, with a preponderance of one over the other depending on moments and circumstances.[129]

Explaining why the *game* component is present in the most elementary manifestations of the divine–human relationship of love would imply first understanding its presence in a delightful human relationship. The notion of *contest* as an element in that relationship is easier to understand, albeit more difficult to fully comprehend the way in which such a complex and mysterious operation comes about. Nevertheless, given the connection between both concepts, one can immediately perceive in the divine–human relationship of love that as soon as the aspect of a *game* appears, even in its simplest forms, therein also, more or less explicitly, is the feature of a *contest*.

The process is similar to what takes place during the diverse phases of development in mystical prayer.

---

[129]It seems impossible to separate the notions of game and contest. The most basic children's games always involve some competitive element with a prize to be won by the winner.

Let us not forget that in prayer Jesus Christ interacts with the soul by means of *human* love through His Human Nature, and, at the same time, by means of *divine* love through His Divine Nature in *one act* of love that has to be attributed, in the last analysis, to His Divine Person because only persons, not natures, love. Therefore, Jesus Christ's act of love for His creature, accomplished within the conditions provided by the Hypostatic Union and the *Communication of Idioms*, can be understood as both *divine love* and *human love*: *divine–human* love; consequently (separable as regards the mode and the object to which it is addressed, but not as regards its origin) offering Jesus Christ the possibility of loving His creature by putting Himself at the creature's level; namely, by loving it in the same and only way in which it knows how to love: none other than in a *human way*.

The creature can only love in a *human way*; elevated and divinized by grace, but always in a human way. And so, the necessary conditions for carrying out the *games of love* have been established for both lovers, Jesus Christ and man.

Now it is possible to imagine as logical that both Lovers allow in their relationship of love such simple, human, and enjoyable things as the child–like game of *hide–and–seek*. For love is not only compatible with *amusement* understood as a manifestation of good cheer, but even demands it as love's primary and elementary constituent. No one could imagine any relationship of love between God and His creature as anything other than a joyful and jubilant one.

General belief, on the contrary, considers the relationship of the creature with God as exclusively unilateral. Prayer becomes a fervent act of worship whereby the soul merely addresses God and thinks of Him as the object of her worship and supplications; this prayer cannot even imagine any kind of relationship (much less a loving relationship) between the soul and God; it is the prayer of Buddhists and Mohammedans. Consequently, multitudes of souls lack the energy to start a prayer life.

Poetry, on the other hand, can easily understand the divine–human relationship of love as being perfectly *human* (which in no way excludes its being perfectly divine) and considers it logical to allow the *ludic* element in this relationship. Thus the Bridegroom hides Himself from the bride, joyfully expecting that she will be able to search Him out and show her longings for Him, or hoping that He may find her first (which is the latent beginning of the *contest* element that is also part of the game):

> *Beloved, I searched to see,*
> *In my orchard, the path where lemon blooms burst,*
> *There I stayed in wait for thee,*
> *Out behind my lemon tree,*
> *To see if, My Beloved, I found you first.*[130]

As actually happens in all games, and in every relationship of love, the bride understands the intentions of the Bridegroom and audaciously answers in kind. The die is cast, and the *game of love* between them begins: You hide and I find you; you run and I reach you; you try to escape and I surprise you; you love me and I love you more... Who would bet on a winner, considering the uncertain outcome of love games? And so the bride answers:

---

[130] *CFC*, 46. In the Spanish original:

> *Amada, yo he buscado*
> *de mi huerto de azahares el sendero,*
> *y luego, te he esperado*
> *detrás del limonero*
> *a ver si te encontraba yo primero.*

My Love, I have walked anew
On your orchard path where lemon blooms have burst.
There I hid myself from you
Behind lemon trees from view
Just to see, My Love, if I could kiss you first.[131]

Once they are together in His orchard, the Bridegroom is ready to make the most of the abundant fruits harvested there, His main pleasure being to enjoy the presence of the bride, along with all the gifts and presents which she offers Him; principal among which is her own love and her own heart.

This coming of the Bridegroom into His orchard to gather the fruits that He anticipates finding there has been captured, as is to be expected, in this passage of the *Song of Songs*; with the particularity that its penetrating and significant meaning transports us to the core of the divine–human union of love and its profound implications for mystic and contemplative prayer:

---

[131] *CFC*, 45. In the Spanish original:

Amado, he recorrido
de tu huerto de azahares el sendero,
y luego, me he escondido
detrás del limonero
a ver si te besaba yo primero.

> *I am come into my garden, O my sister, my spouse,*
> *I have gathered my myrrh, with my aromatical spices;*
> *I have eaten the honeycomb with my honey,*
> *I have drunk my wine with my milk.*
> *Eat, O friends, and drink, and be inebriated,*
>   *my dearly beloved.*[132]

The description of the fruits that the Bridegroom hopes to harvest is so rich that its meaning goes unnoticed by most commentators. The Bridegroom comes to His garden *to gather His myrrh and His aromatical spices, to eat the honeycomb with His honey, to drink His wine with His milk.* It must be noted that the fruits found in the garden are the goods offered to Him by the bride, beginning with her own person, which is why the Bridegroom *gathers them.*

Once again, as in passing, the different identities of the Bridegroom and of the bride are brought to the fore, now reaffirmed by the contrast between what He offers and what she gives. Let us not forget that reciprocity is the quality that best expresses the existence of an *I* and a *thou* in the relationship of love between lovers.

It also is noteworthy that the Bridegroom invites his friends to come and enjoy and drink with Him till they

---

[132]Sg 5:1.

become *inebriated*; a meaningful term suggesting, in the best imaginable way, the mystery of the superabundant and ineffable reality that love is and of the immensity of the divine–human relationship of love. The comparison between this relationship and a merely human one is purely analogical, so to speak; therefore, the depth of the former is accessible only to those who have known God, for this is the *only way* of gaining insight into the true meaning of love: *He that loveth not, knoweth not God; for God is love;*[133] which is tantamount to saying that *he who does not love God, cannot love; for God is love.* This is how the existence of millions of human beings has been spent: without knowing Love and not living Life.

If the love relationship of the creature with God, according to this passage of the *Song of Songs*, is a veritable contest or *tournament of love*, then he who begins on the road of contemplative prayer must be willing to embark on a risky undertaking in which he will have to confront a *serious and demanding challenge.*

The language that describes the events of the relationship of the creature with God is not figurative speech nor does it depict pretended attitudes. This means that this language speaks of acts of love because true love is there; it

---

[133] 1 Jn 4:8.

refers to a contest or a fight because we are dealing with a *true* combat. In the latter example one can affirm with total certainty that both contestants are urged to take each other on.

According to this, the soul that is willing to go deeper into mystical prayer should know that she must confront a true *challenge.*

What is at stake in this joust or combat is love itself, therefore the consequence is obvious. We are not dealing here with an ostentatious display; the weaker contestant is not going to receive advantages or special considerations; nor is anybody going to speculate about circumstances favorable to the stronger challenger. If either of the contenders, especially the less–abled one (the human soul in this case) feels courageous enough to accept the challenge, he *will also have to put up with all the consequences.*[134]

We are talking about a true *challenge* as the very words of Jesus Christ clearly confirm:

---

[134]This circumstance, like many others, has not been sufficiently taken into account throughout the History of Spirituality; in itself it would suffice to deter anybody from accepting the contest; which would be a pitiful decision made without giving consideration to two things: the grandeur and wonder of what is involved in this challenge (which in itself deserves the risk), and the special circumstances of this contest, for God would never put the soul to an impossible test or to a trial which at any moment lacks the sense of fairness.

If any man will come after me, let him deny himself, and take up his cross, and follow me.[135]

Every one of you that doth not renounce all that he possesseth, cannot be my disciple.[136]

If any man come to me, and hate not his father, and mother, and wife, and children, and brethren, and sisters, yea and his own life also, he cannot be my disciple.[137]

Whosoever will save his life, shall lose it: and whosoever shall lose his life for my sake and the gospel, shall save it.[138]

And He said to one who was willing to follow Him:

The foxes have holes, and the birds of the air nests; but the Son of man hath not where to lay his head.[139]

There is an ensuing question from what we have said about love being a *veritable joust or tournament* and the reality most seriously contemplated in Revelation: given the evident disparity of power, could there be a possibility for the creature to win the combat?

---

[135] Mt 16:24.

[136] Lk 14:33.

[137] Lk 14:26.

[138] Mk 8:35.

[139] Lk 9:58.

And the answer, which cannot strike us as strange, has to be in the affirmative.

There are scriptural texts that support this statement:

First, the mysterious story of Genesis 32: 25–30, in which Jacob fought with an Angel; later the text tells us that this Angel is God and that He was defeated by Jacob. There are many interpretations of this text, but none is completely satisfactory. In fact, it is an inspired text, contained in the Book of Genesis; and it is well known that God does not speak lightly or simply for the sake of talking.

In the New Testament we have as precedents the parables of the talents and of the pounds. In them some servants who received goods of their lord negotiated with them during his absence and were able to give him back *even double* the amount received.

Given the way in which this issue has been dealt with in the *Song of Songs* —supported by other biblical texts— thus considering that the relationship of love between the soul and Jesus Christ follows the pattern of a *tournament of love* with all the conditions already explained, one may ask if there is a possibility that God could be defeated by His creature in the field of love.

We have anticipated our answer in the affirmative, endorsed by the above–mentioned text of Genesis and the parables of the talents and of the pounds. *The problem begins in earnest when one tries to explain why and how this victory of the creature can be attained.*

To find some sort of an answer, one would have to delve into the deepest recesses of the mysterious divine–human relationship of love. As anyone can understand, this is impossible; except when man is assisted by a special divine help that offers him *some* approach to this mystery.

But, as we have said before, it would not make any sense to divine intelligence and goodness that God should reveal to man unintelligible notions that can never be deciphered. Besides, the end of Revelation is nothing other than the salvation of man; therefore, one can very well presume that God would want to give us at least *some intimation* of the mystery along with His words; an intimation which is sufficient enough to contribute not only to the salvation and consolation of our souls, but also to our sharing, even now, in God's bounteous and marvelous gifts.

The first step in approaching the content of this mystery could be to examine the similarities and differences between the contest of a real fight and the contest of love. A careful consideration of the different circumstances of these two kinds of contests can shed light upon incredible scenes which, while moving us to think of unknown, fantastic worlds, will show the ineffable grandeur, beauty, heroism, overflowing generosity, and self–renunciation involved in the vigorous attempts carried out by one challenger in the contest of love to surpass the love of his counterpart.

In real combat the desire to defeat the adversary prevails over everything else.

In the tournament of love, by contrast, each contender is filled with great longing to love the other more and more. Consequently, the combat is fought not overshadowed by the fear of being defeated but under the mantle of an indescribable joy brought about by the following circumstances:

In the first place, the very act of contending over love with the beloved, which brings about an overflowing and ineffable joy that love alone, the direct fruit of the Holy Spirit, can cause. Therefore, the combat and contest out of love is in itself capable of plunging the soul into an ocean of joy similar to the bliss she will end up having in Heaven.

On the other hand, the soul that contends with Jesus Christ for love certainly desires to overpower Him in love, if such a thing were possible; but this is not as important to the soul as *pleasing* her Beloved, so much so that she would wish herself to be defeated if her being vanquished would bring pleasure to Him Whom she loves.[140]

---

[140] As one can understand, all these circumstances and many others, totally unknown to most Christians, would be sufficient enough to dispel any sanctimonious fear of prayer and to foster one's desire to set out to tread the paths of mystical prayer.

In real combat, the contenders are bent on achieving victory to obtain a merely human triumphal wreath.

In the tournament of love, however, the awareness of having attained victory is totally irrelevant to both contenders:

First, because each one would be overtaken by joy were he to contemplate *the victory of the other.* Love is like that, it wants only the good and the joy of the beloved.

Second, it could happen that the Divine Bridegroom may feel Himself completely *captured and crushed* by the relentless love of the bride. This frequently happens to souls very advanced in their spiritual lives. In these circumstances the Bridegroom considers Himself *ravished and held captive* by the love strings of the bride:

> *Thou hast wounded my heart, my sister, my spouse,*
> *Thou hast wounded my heart with one of thy eyes,*
> *And with one hair of thy neck.*[141]

It is possible then that, at some point, the Bridegroom, due to the fervent love of the bride and her unreserved self–giving, may feel Himself wounded by love and voluntarily surrender, *defeated,* to the bride.

---

[141] Sg 4:9.

> *If I found myself with you in Love's contest,*
> *Drenched in blood and unable to defeat you,*
> *The helmet lost; likewise, broken is the crest,*
> *My soul, even to death, blindly loving you,*
> *Defeated, crushed, I would decide and attest*
> *That rendered by your love, I belong to you.*[142]

This *surrendering* of the Bridegroom is, of course, voluntary, as expressed in the verse which states that *He, having surrendered to the bride's love, has decided to belong to her*; which does not diminish in the least the true nature of His surrender and the character of authentic acknowledgement of the bride's victory over Him.

But, at the same time, the bride feels herself *defeated* and utterly confused by the generous act of love of the Bridegroom, to Whom she rightly concedes true victory. And the Bridegroom, in turn, also considers the victory of

---

[142] *CFC*, 104. In the Spanish original:

> *Si al batirme contigo yo me viera,*
> *teñido en sangre, sin poder vencerte,*
> *perdido el casco, rota la cimera,*
> *ciega por ti mi alma hasta la muerte,*
> *vencido y derrotado decidiera,*
> *rendido por tu amor, pertenecerte.*

the bride as His own, because to Him belongs everything
that is hers, and He alone has brought her to this situation.

In this way it is possible to contemplate in the divine–
human *contest of love* the incredible reality of both contestants being at one and the same time both victor and vanquished. Let us remember that when we speak of victory
it is a *true victory*, and it is a *true defeat* when we speak of
defeat. Indeed, God finds no pleasure in structuring His
relationship of love with His creature upon *theatrical* or
fabricated attitudes that have little to do with reality.

Now the bride realizes that her race has been completed and she sees her joy consummated in the arms of
her Bridegroom:

> *And there my ended woes and sorrows left me*
> *There where our lives are joined as one, by the sea*
> *Rocked with gentle waves created easily*
> *By the stirred blue waters lapping lazily.*[143]

---

[143] *CFC*, 105. In the Spanish original:

> *Y allí mis penas fueron fenecidas*
> *junto al mar que vio unidas nuestras vidas,*
> *mecido en suaves ondas,*
> *producidas por las azules aguas removidas.*

Despite the efforts made by the soul to identify her own life with the life of Jesus Christ by practicing asceticism and a serious prayer life, she cannot attain complete union with Him if she has not previously detached herself from all that she owns: *every one of you that doth not renounce all that he possesseth, cannot be my disciple.*[144]

The doctrine of Saint John of the Cross concerning this topic emphasizes that the soul needs to abandon and get rid of everything created and any gift received, including her own thoughts and sentiments, the faculties of the soul, and the external and internal senses. He also teaches that the soul must do away with —even reject— all memories, any elaborated concept of God, locutions or visions received from Him (no matter how authentic they may be), and even the very idea of the Humanity of Christ. Only in this way, Saint John would say, is it possible for the soul to reach complete union with God Who transcends all human thought and created things.

As we have said several times in this essay, this doctrine seems difficult and radical.

But it is not in the least our intention to challenge the doctrine of this Saint Doctor of the Church. We do not rule out the possibility that we have not understood

---

[144]Lk 14:33.

his teaching or have not assimilated some of its points. Be that as it may, we will underline some topics of his doctrine that are difficult to accept or at least incompatible with what we have explained about mystical prayer.

As anyone will have realized by now, our expounding on mystical prayer does not follow the line of thought of the mystical Doctor which stresses the *annihilation of the faculties of the soul and the elimination of their operations* in order to attain full union with the transcendent God.

Nevertheless, we must completely coincide with the Saint on this point, namely the need to renounce everything one has if one wants to achieve complete union with Jesus Christ.

But we disagree on *the way in which this is to be accomplished.*

While the Saint argues for the absolute *elimination* of all things in order to arrive at the union of love, we favor *keeping them* in order to *offer them* to the Bridegroom, thus making possible our relationship of love with Him.

The Saint simply *eliminates* them. We, on the contrary, *give them* as an offering of love to the Bridegroom, as we use the goods and faculties that we have received (which are inherent in human nature) to interact with Him. In this way, the final outcome being absolutely *identical* —renouncing all things out of love for Jesus Christ—, the way of going about it is, nonetheless, *different.*

Truly speaking, our procedure, path to be followed, and way of using God's gifts have little to do with Saint John's method.

The bride of the *Song of Songs* seems to think as we do in our exposition:

> *The mandrakes yield their fragrance,*
> *The most exquisite fruits are at our doors;*
> *The new as well as the old,*
> *I have stored them for you, my love.*[145]

...for she clearly keeps the fruits of her orchard in store to offer them to her Bridegroom.[146]

The Bridegroom of the *Song* also seems to agree with our approach:

> *I am come into my garden, O my sister, my spouse,*
> *I have gathered my myrrh, with my aromatical spices;*
> *I have eaten the honeycomb with my honey,*
> *I have drunk my wine with my milk.*
> *Eat, O friends, and drink, and be inebriated,*
>   *my dearly beloved.*[147]

---

[145] Sg 7:14.

[146] Evidently, we have to distinguish, on the one hand, between the totality of things abandoned to set out in the following of Jesus Christ with the possibility of reaching high degrees of prayer, and, on the other, the sentiments and faculties of the soul, which are indispensable to our relationship with God.

[147] Sg 5:1.

It would be difficult to consider the relationship of love between the Bridegroom and the bride —which, after all, is a nuptial relationship: *Blessed are they that are called to the marriage supper of the Lamb*—[148] while disregarding the elements of feast and joy, as well as the mutual interchange of gifts, involved in it.

In the process of mystical prayer, the bride needs to hear the voice of the Bridegroom, for a relationship between lovers cannot be conceived in any other way:

> *Come to me; be with me; stay.*
> *While brisk North winds gust over the high meadow;*
> *Leave the flock to find its way,*
> *Whisper to me, faint and low,*
> *That you feel wounded by my love's tender blow.*[149]

It is difficult to imagine an obscure sort of *unilateral* worship in which the bride cannot but negate what she has, including the faculties of the soul, and not expect for

---

[148]Rev 19:9.

[149] *CFC*, 59. In the Spanish original:

> *Acércate a mi lado*
> *mientras el cierzo sopla en el egido,*
> *y deja ya el ganado,*
> *y cuéntame al oído*
> *si acaso por mi amor estás herido.*

the present to receive any manifestations of reciprocating love (should she receive them, she would be compelled to reject them).

And according to our system of thought, the Bridegroom also needs to hear the voice of the bride and contemplate her face:

> *Shew me thy face, let thy voice sound in my ears;*
> *For thy voice is sweet, and thy face comely.*[150]

If the soul had to completely abandon the idea of the Humanity of Christ it would be impossible to understand the process of her relationship of love with the Bridegroom, for, as we have said repeatedly, man cannot but love in a *human way*; it would also be impossible to grasp the bride's attempt to describe the Bridegroom:

> *My beloved is white and ruddy,*
> *Chosen out of thousands.*
> *His head is as the finest gold,*
> *His locks as branches of palm trees,*
> *Black as a raven.*
> *His eyes as doves upon brooks of waters,*
> *Which are washed with milk,*
> *And sit beside the plentiful streams.*[151]

---

[150]Sg 2:14.

[151]Sg 5: 10–12.

Beautiful and poetic metaphors, some would say. Indeed, they are. But even if one grants that these expressions are only shadowy evocations and approximations,
how else could the bride describe the Bridegroom? If human language cannot be used to express the sentiments
of the soul or attempt to draw a picture of what is absolutely impossible to describe, what other language could
be employed? Poetry and its figures of speech (such as
metaphors, metonymy, synecdoche, and all others) are re-
sources and consolations to which man can resort in order
to palliate the poverty and limitations of his language.

To some people, for whom the *Song of Songs* is simply a number of epithalamic and merely human songs, the
texts which we have been quoting here to support our speculations prove absolutely nothing; which must be granted
to them, should they have lost their faith and no longer
believe the words of Scripture. But that opinion is totally
erroneous for those who have kept their belief in the revealed Word of God and faithfully accept the truth of the
words of the Books as inspired by the Holy Spirit. In effect, God has spoken to man to tell him something. And
if the Holy Spirit has used poetry in Books like the *Song
of Songs*, He did so not with the intention to brag about
being a good poet but to contribute to man's salvation
with an adequate language; the very language demanded

at the moment by the magnitude of the theme and the non–existence of any better means of expression.

It is said that one needs to renounce the operations of the three faculties of the soul —intellect, memory, and will— and one's elaborated ideas about God and similar sentiments as the only acceptable means to reaching total emptiness of the soul, which, in turn, is the one and only way to attain union with the totally transcendent God.

But Jesus Christ kept the faculties of His soul and His human emotions intact until the last moment of His death on the Cross: He begged His Father to intervene in favor of His executioners; He forgave the Good Thief; He commended His Mother to the care and protection of His disciple John; He breathed His last, commending His Spirit into the hands of His Father...[152]

Otherwise, it would be difficult to comprehend the possibility and development of the relationship of divine–human love, without which the possibility of mystical and contemplative prayer also vanishes. How could one express the longing of the search; the urgency of the waiting caused by the absence of the beloved Bridegroom when

---

[152]He also kept all his human faculties and sentiments, as well as the wounds of His Body, after His Resurrection. According to Saint Paul, those who, after the Resurrection of the Flesh, have attained salvation will enjoy a glorious body similar to the glorious Body of Christ.

it seems that He is never going to arrive; the joy of the meeting; the bliss brought about by the sentiments experienced in the intimacy of the divine–human relationship of love; the wonder experienced by God and His creature following their mutual contemplation as lovers?

If Jesus Christ is our life, as Saint Paul says (Col 3:4), to renounce the idea of the Humanity of Jesus Christ (that is, of Jesus Christ)[153] in order to attain union with the Godhead would be to renounce our life, the meaning of our existence, and any intimation of what Perfect Joy could mean for us. If to attain perfection in contemplative prayer one needs to walk along the road not thinking of Him, I, on my part, would not even be willing to begin the journey.

6. By Way of Epilogue

Having reached this point, I think I must conclude my undertaking. Not because I have finished it, but because

---

[153] Jesus Christ without His Humanity, or without His divinity, is not Jesus Christ. The Incarnate Word is True God and True Man. Two Natures, Divine and Human, inseparably and indissolubly united to the one Divine Person of the Word.

nothing can be considered completed if one does not even have the certainty of having begun it.

Speaking about mystic or contemplative prayer is an undertaking which nobody knows how to begin, much less how to unfold it; finding a way to complete such a task would be something absolutely impossible. Besides, one must have a good background in and deep knowledge of this issue and, what is more important, a knowledge acquired through significant experience in it. I do not possess either, for I lack any mystical experience.

Therefore, I agree that writing about mystical prayer has been quite daring on my part. But without audacity many initiatives undertaken by man would never have been accomplished. True, a great number of them ended up in failure; but those which culminated in success are sufficient enough to justify human boldness. As for the particular risk I have undergone in writing this essay, I must admit that I do not care much about the results; I am simply satisfied with the intentions which have compelled me to complete this job.

I felt encouraged to write this because of my confidence in the content of Sacred Scripture and in the readings of the mystics and spiritual authors. But my firm trust would never have been enough —of this much I am sure— had I not relied on another element which, in the end, became essential: the sentiment that something wonderful and indescribable —whose origin was completely unknown to me, for I could not discern it— was compelling me to set about this task. This something aroused in me the distinctive *feeling* that right there was what my heart had always been looking for but never attained. I could not explain it then; neither can I now. That *something* mysteriously awoke in my soul feelings hitherto unknown to me which revealed to me the unavoidable necessity of knowing love and experiencing Perfect Joy. Those feelings even seemed to provide me with a strange light which uncovered for me in the way of infinite horizons a truth I had never before dreamed of.

In the weak light shed by this just–mentioned feeling, the end appeared beyond my reach, and the way leading to it seemed to predict an almost impossible journey for any beginner. And yet, the feelings which filled my soul were so strong that it seemed as if they wanted to talk to me and encourage me to undertake the adventure.

These reasons may not seem sufficient to make this task reasonable; but they were for me. Besides, I was overtaken by the enthusiastic idea that this work may encourage someone to set out on the paths of prayer; especially since the description of those paths provided here do not resemble much the solemn, stodgy, and dry lucubration of treatises which turn prayer into something exclusively for penitents, hermits, and contemplative nuns of distant past.

This is the reason I have introduced a variety of poetic fragments. Very few of them belong to Saint John of the Cross; the rest are mine. Possibly the Saint has felt uncomfortable (although in Heaven there is no room for displeasure or sadness) because his incomparable stanzas have been quoted in a book alongside others of medium quality. But the poetry of the Saint from Fontiveros is extremely well–known and abundantly quoted; as for mine, if truth be told, I can only say that I had nothing else more appropriate for the task at hand.

I am convinced, nevertheless, that they bring into this work a relative sense of beauty and an environment of joy and light that are, after all, so necessary in a world that has seemingly opted for ugliness and darkness. Besides, we need to introduce poetry into the treatises on prayer and to the ideas about prayer held by average Christians (including many religious men and women —when they used to pray, that is).

Finally, as kind readers will understand, I have been encouraged to write this work solely by the good will and enthusiasm that God so frequently puts into our hearts.

First, as I have said, from the desire that this work may provide the occasion for some souls to feel keen about beginning the practice of prayer or to improve it with more enthusiasm. The great number of good souls who day after day make an effort to not miss their prayer but make no further advancement —for they think that this is not possible— along the possibly difficult but wonderful ways that lead to intimacy with Jesus Christ is one of the things that probably brings about the most sadness in God when He sees the Flock of His Church.

Secondly, because I for one have felt, as I was writing this work, thrills and longings about what is said in it; and I have desired that at least some of the beauty that this work may have would become real in my soul. As for the rest, despite being immersed in the midst of so many vicissitudes and numerous ups and downs, my soul has always been filled with longings and dreams about God. Longings and thrills dreamt of but not always accompanied by sufficient efforts and, therefore, never attained. But the just man lives by faith, as Saint Paul affirmed, and he is also sustained by hope. A hope that in itself suffices to give us a pledge of Perfect Joy and to keep lit in our hearts the light which assures us that one day, perhaps at the moment least expected, Perfect Love will knock at our door.

And in giving up the labor now as done,
His task neither consummated nor begun
The bard sighed in his sorrow and fell silent:
Who would dare to sing to Beauty his lament?
And praise with words its grandeur so transcendent...?
And finally, with hurried pace he left then
His quill he left behind, it was forgotten.[154]

---

[154] *CFC*, 124. In the Spanish original:

Y dando la labor por terminada,
ni consumada ni aun menos empezada,
el bardo enmudeció, no sin tristeza:
¿Mas quién podrá cantar a la Belleza
y loar con palabras su grandeza...?
Y fuese al fin, en marcha apresurada,
dejando atrás su péñola olvidada.

Index of Quotations
from the
New Testament

MATTHEW

7: 8, **124**
14, **44**, **108**
10: 39, **45**, **136**
15: 27, **125**
16: 24, **164**
25, **45**

MARK

8: 35, **164**
10: 45, **146**
52, **125**
13: 31, **56**

LUKE

1: 34, **137**
9: 58, **164**
11: 10, **124**
14: 26, **45**, **164**
33, **164**, **171**
21: 33, **56**

JOHN

1: 5, **102**
18, **144**
3: 8, **136**
10: 10, **64**
12: 24, **108**
14: 6, **56**, **112**
15: 15, **49**, **146**

ACTS OF THE APOSTLES

20: 35, **151**

ROMANS

4: 18, **80**
6: 3, **95**
8: 26, **35**, **62**
12: 15, **104**
14: 7-8, **95**, **152**

1 CORINTHIANS

12: 3, **129**
13: 10, **48**

2 CORINTHIANS

12: 2–4, **29**

GALATIANS

5: 22, **126**

EPHESIANS

3: 18–19, **61**

PHILIPPIANS

1: 21, **74**
   23–24, **34**
2: 5–8, **145**

COLOSSIANS

3: 4, **178**

2 TIMOTHY

3: 12, **108**

HEBREWS

12: 29, **35**, **70**, **139**
13: 8, **70**

2 PETER

1: 19, **41**

1 JOHN

2: 22–23, **57**
4: 8, **43**, **44**, **162**
   19, **60**, **116**

REVELATION

3: 20, **143**
19: 9, **174**
22: 13, **154**

Table of Contents

The Mystery of Prayer

Preliminary Note of the Author 9

First Part
Introduction

1. Introduction 15
2. Contemplative Prayer 23
3. Conclusion 78

Second Part
Structure of Mystical Prayer

1. Prolegomena 87
2. About the doctrinal authority of the Spanish Mystics
   and the meaning of these Contributions 91
3. Diverse approaches regarding the indispensability of
   the cross and purification in mystical prayer 93
4. Contemplative prayer from the point of view of the
   Song of Songs and mystic poetry. Necessary antece-
   dents 100
5. The divine–human relationship of love throughout our
   way of attaining contemplative prayer 115
6. By Way of Epilogue 178